Let's Learn Logistics Through Simulation – Aprendamos Logística a Través de la Simulación

Future of Education – Futuro de la Educación

Eds. María Soledad Ramírez-Montoya, Rasikh Tariq, Leonardo David Glasserman Morales, Edgar Omar López-Caudana & Inés Alvarez-Icaza Longoria

VOL. 4

María Soledad Ramírez-Montoya, Ernesto Armando Pacheco-Velázquez,
Leonardo David Glasserman Morales, Virginia Rodés Paragarino,
Carolina Alcántar-Nieblas, Pamela Geraldine Olivo Montaño &
Fidel Antonio Guadalupe Casillas Muñoz

Let's Learn Logistics Through Simulation – Aprendamos Logística a Través de la Simulación

S4L Platform – Plataforma S4L

PETER LANG

Berlin · Bruxelles · Chennai · Lausanne · New York · Oxford

Bibliographic Information published by the Deutsche Nationalbibliothek
The Deutsche Nationalbibliothek lists this publication in the Deutsche Nationalbibliografie; detailed bibliographic data is available online at http://dnb.d-nb.de.

Library of Congress Cataloging-in-Publication Data
A CIP catalog record for this book has been applied for at the Library of Congress.

Cover Credit: Michael Haderer, Vienna, Austria

ISSN 3053-4593 (Print) | 3053-4607 (Online)
ISBN 978-3-631-93305-3 (Print)
ISBN 978-3-631-93314-5 (ePDF)
ISBN 978-3-631-93315-2 (ePUB)
DOI 10.3726/b22874

info@peterlang.com

Published by Peter Lang GmbH, Berlin, Germany

This publication has been peer reviewed.

www.peterlang.com

Contact for General Product Safety Regulation (GPSR): gpsr@peterlang.com

Table of Contents

ENGLISH

Let's Learn Logistics Through Simulation

S4L Platform

Figure 1.
IRG-R4C Researchers, mobilisers of the S4L platform

About Us

We are members of the IRG-R4C Interdisciplinary Research Group Scaling Complex Thinking for All (Figure 1). We are passionate about taking higher education to new levels of excellence. We are dedicated to developing and promoting advanced reasoning competencies to face the complexity of the modern world. We use open science strategies and the most advanced 5.0 technologies, such as artificial intelligence and data science, to create training systems that prepare people for the challenges of the future. Our work is linked to projects that integrate universities, industries, the government and the civil sector, always seeking sustainable solutions that benefit the whole society.

Our vision is clear and ambitious: to contribute meaningfully to the future of education, creating innovative solutions to the problems and challenges of today's society. We align with the goals of UNESCO's 2030 Agenda for Sustainable Development, fostering interdisciplinary collaboration and building robust academic networks. At IRG-R4C, we work to train a new generation of highly competitive professionals committed to social welfare who always seek to enable innovative solutions that respond to present and future challenges.

Editorial Letter

We are excited to share with you our vision to design an innovative educational platform that acts as a learning content management system, from which the creation, management and distribution of educational content is facilitated. This platform validates the development of reasoning competencies for complexity and self-regulated learning in its users, including students, academic staff, decision-makers and representatives of the business sector. Our objective is to support the training of professionals who are capable of facing lifelong learning needs and to prepare them for current and future challenges.

The S4L (Simulation for Learning) project is significant because it seeks to promote competitiveness in the logistics industry, with training instances that allow people to make decisions more efficiently. This approach not only improves individual skills but also contributes to the development of the sector. Users of the platform can acquire knowledge in a playful way, observe the consequences of each decision, identify the main variables that influence real processes and develop an intrinsic motivation to investigate, understand and experiment with new strategies that optimise problem solving. The impact targets of this project are governments, professional associations, NGOs and the business sector.

We invite you to participate in a platform that transforms the way we learn and solve problems, preparing us for a brighter and more efficient future!

OBJECTIVES

Our main goal is to develop a learning content management system platform that, using Industry 5.0 tools such as cloud computing, artificial intelligence, simulations, serious games, biometrics, data analytics and open resources, promotes complex reasoning and self-regulated learning skills. This platform provides quantitative and qualitative indicators on user behaviour to train professionals who are capable of adapting and learning continuously, providing adequate preparation for the challenges of a constantly changing world.

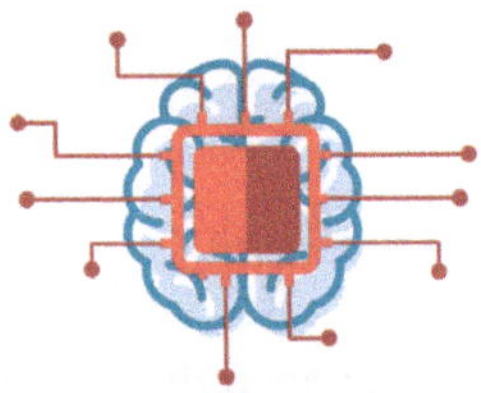

SPECIFIC OBJECTIVES

1. Select, with an interdisciplinary team, the essential characteristics that guarantee that the platform promotes the development of specific skills, such as complex thinking. This allows you to properly configure your design and architecture.

2. To analyse the operation of the first version of the platform to determine its effectiveness in the development of complex reasoning and self-regulated learning. The selected instruments are used for the participant's performance evaluation, and based on the results, the experience of the users will be assessed to make improvements.

3. Validate the platform with strategic partners and register the platform's intellectual property. Finally, a process of technology transference is carried out to various sectors and stakeholders.

Figure 2.
General and specific objectives of the S4L platform

Objectives

Introduction

In the 1980s, I watched a movie starring Tom Hanks called 'I Wish I Were Big'. In this film, the main character, Josh Baskin, is a child trapped in the body of an adult. This character dreams of an interactive game in which participants can change or create characters, by giving them different characteristics and creating their own stories. The creation of software that allows people to build different stories, just by changing a few details in the characterisation of the participants, can be a way to materialise Josh Baskin's dream.

For many years, I have dedicated my time to teaching decision-making in the logistics field, and I have always considered logistics to be a game of strategy wherein every choice impacts the final result. Just like in a game, logistics managers must consider multiple variables, such as supplier selection, factory locations, distribution centres and store management. Each decision must be carefully analysed and adjusted in response to changes in the environment (Kong, 2021). For example, a strategy player must adapt their moves to overcome challenges and achieve their goals. When the characteristics of some of the variables change, it is quite possible that the results obtained by following a certain strategy will also change.

The research project Simulation for Learning (S4L) served as the starting point for developing the logistics simulation platform called V-Logistics. Through S4L, experiential learning methods in virtual environments were explored to enhance understanding and decision-making in logistics. The findings and methodologies designed within S4L laid the groundwork for creating V-Logistics, a tool that enables users to model and simulate 3D logistics environments. The relationship between the two is fundamental, as V-Logistics applies S4L principles by offering an interactive simulation environment optimised for learning and practice in logistics, thereby promoting knowledge transfer through realistic simulated experiences.

The project was born from the need to address the limitations of traditional teaching methods in logistics, which are often too theoretical and do not reflect the complexity and dynamism of the real world. Our innovation seeks to fill this gap by providing a tool that simulates a real logistics environment, allowing each student to learn by doing and adapt to different scenarios and challenges.

'V-Logistics' is an educational platform that allows participants to design and manage their own logistics chain. This platform lets users to choose the line of business; define the number of suppliers, factories, distribution centres and stores; and customise the characteristics of each of these elements (Pacheco-Velázquez et al., 2023). The idea is that each participant can experience and learn about logistics in a practical and dynamic way, like how Josh, the main character of 'How I Got Big', imagined his game.

The Simulation for Learning (S4L) project emerged with the vision of contributing to the survival of small businesses and the quality of life of the inhabitants, collaborating with different actors of society for the creation of various scenarios according to the reality of each region (Figure 3). The main objective of our project, represented through the V-Logistics platform, is to improve each person's understanding and skills in logistics and optimisation by offering an interactive and personalised learning experience. We hope that those who participate will not only acquire theoretical knowledge but also develop practical skills when facing real situations and making decisions that affect the performance of their logistics chain.

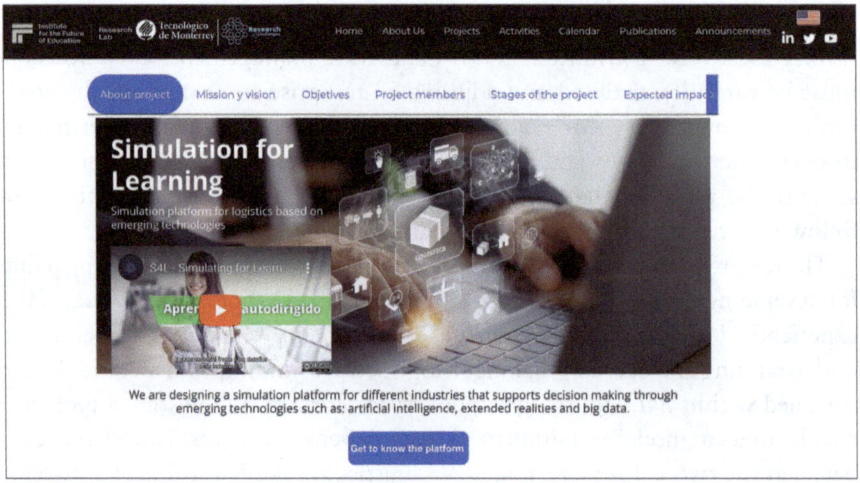

Figure 3. S4L project website (https://www.research4challenges.world/en/s4l-1)

The relevance of this proposal is based on research that underlines the importance of experiential learning and gamification in education. Studies* have shown that more information is retained, and better skills are developed when one actively participates in the learning process. By offering a learning environment in which an individual can experiment and learn from their own decisions, our software effectively addresses the problems of disconnection between theory and practice that have persisted in the teaching of logistics. It will benefit diverse groups of learners, including those with special needs or in disadvantaged contexts, by providing an accessible tool that is adaptable to different learning styles and skill levels. Students will be able to see in real time how their decisions impact the logistics chain, fostering deep and meaningful learning.

Our project has the potential to transform education in logistics, providing an innovative tool that combines theory and practice in an interactive way. The customisation and flexibility offered by the platform not only enhances the learning experience but also prepares people to face real-world challenges. The importance of continuing to innovate in education is crucial to preparing new generations for an increasingly complex and dynamic future.

References

Kong, Y. (2021). The role of experiential learning on students' motivation and classroom engagement. *Frontiers in Psychology*, https://doi.org/10.3389/fpsyg.2021.771272

Pacheco-Velázquez, E., Salinas-Navarro, D. E., & Ramírez-Montoya, M. S. (2023). Serious Games and Experiential Learning: Options for Engineering Education. *International Journal of Serious Games*, 10(3), 3–21 https://doi.org/10.17083/ijsg.v10i3.593

How is Complex Thinking Linked to Logistics Processes?

Complex thinking is a skill that allows us to see problems and situations from a broad and interconnected perspective. Instead of breaking everything down into isolated parts, it helps us understand how all the pieces of a system relate to and influence each other. It's like seeing an entire forest instead of just looking tree by tree. This approach combines different ways of thinking: seeing patterns (systemic), basing on facts and evidence (scientific), critically analysing (critical) and finding creative solutions (innovative). By adopting complex thinking, we can make more informed and effective decisions in any aspect of our lives.

Now, imagine applying this powerful combination in the field of logistics. Logistics involves efficiently planning, implementing and controlling the flow and storage of goods, services and information from origin to consumption, ensuring customer satisfaction. Using complex thinking in logistics means seeing the entire process as an interconnected system, using data and evidence to make decisions, constantly evaluating strategies and always looking for innovative ways to improve.

The competence of complex thinking is revealed as fundamental in the development of skills for logistics, a field that requires the effective management of multiple interconnected variables in real time. In logistics, complex thinking allows professionals to understand and optimise the supply chain from a holistic perspective and enables them to anticipate how changes in one area may impact others. For example, it can help predict the effect of a transportation delay on inventory levels or customer satisfaction, facilitating quick and informed decisions. This integrative approach not only improves operational efficiency, but also empowers the ability to innovate in the creation of logistics solutions that adapt to emerging challenges, such as market fluctuations or global disruptions.

TO KNOW MORE …

On Complex Thinking and Logistics Processes

Thinking about Complexity. Crisis and Metamorphosis

Author: Edgar Morin

Reference: Morin, E. (2010). *Thinking about complexity. Crisis and metamorphosis.* University of Valencia.

▶ Today, I invite you to discover an exciting study that connects complex thinking with logistics processes – two areas that, combined, can transform our understanding and the management of the world. Complex thinking helps us see the connections and interactions between various parts of a system, allowing us to approach problems with a comprehensive and multidisciplinary vision. Now, imagine applying this way of thinking to logistics, where we plan and control the flow of goods, services and information. To delve deeper into this fascinating perspective, we invite you to read 'Thinking about complexity. Crisis and Metamorphosis' by Edgar Morin. This book is a window into Morin's transdisciplinary thinking, which combines knowledge from various disciplines, such as physics, biology and ethics. Its innovative approach teaches us to see beyond the silos of knowledge and to understand the complexity of social and natural phenomena.

Exploring Educational Simulation Platform Features for Addressing Complexity in Industry 4.0: A Qualitative Analysis of Insights from Logistics Experts

Authors: Ernesto Pacheco-Velazquez, Virginia Rodés Paragarino & Alberto Márquez-Uribe

Reference: Pacheco-Velazquez, E., Rodés, V., & Alberto Márquez-Uribe. 2023. Exploring Educational Simulation Platform Features for Addressing Complexity in Industry 4.0: A Qualitative Analysis of Insights from Logistics Experts. Frontiers in Education. https://doi.org/10.3389/feduc.2024.1331911 https://repositorio.tec.mx/handle/11285/652447

▶ To learn more about this topic, we recommend this fabulous study that examines how Industry 4.0, with technologies such as artificial intelligence and big data analytics, is transforming industrial operations and logistics, highlighting the challenges and need for new tools to manage complexity. Through the design and use of logistics simulators adapted to Industry 4.0, the aim of our project is to equip professionals with the necessary skills to improve decision-making and operational planning in this technologically advanced environment.

Open Model of Complex Thinking for the Future of Education

Authors: María Soledad Ramírez-Montoya, Fabián Eduardo Basabe, Martina Carlos Arroyo, Irma Azeneth Patiño Zúñiga, I. A. & May Portuguez Castro

Reference: Ramírez-Montoya, M. S., Basabe, E., Carlos Arroyo, M., Patiño Zúñiga, I. A., Portuguez Castro, M. (2024). *Open model of complex thinking for the future of education.* Octahedron. https://hdl.handle.net/11285/652033

▶ To discover more about complex thinking, we invite you to explore this text, which presents an innovative educational approach. This approach is designed to respond to the demands of the modern world, integrating the following dimensions of thinking: critical, scientific, systemic and innovative. The objective is to train empathetic citizens who are committed to sustainable development. This model is applied in academic environments, the government and business sectors, highlighting the importance of collaboration, empathy and commitment to sustainable solutions to global problems. By immersing yourself in this approach, you will be able to develop skills that will allow you to contribute meaningfully to society and the well-being of the planet.

Educational Innovation in Action

The V-Logistics platform is an educational tool that transforms the way we teach and learn about logistics, operations and supply chains. Use specific case studies and scenarios to improve important skills, such as complex thinking and autonomous learning. This platform not only presents information but also helps users develop and sharpen their critical competencies through practice and interaction with relevant content.

V-Logistics is characterised by the following:

- Multimodal educational content: Includes a wide range of teaching materials, such as videos, tutorials, infographics and interactive resources. Open access is promoted, as some materials are generated as open educational resources (OER). Resources are available in Spanish and English.
- Assessments and progress tracking: Allows users to assess their understanding of content and progress with respect to the development of complex thinking skills and self-regulated learning through online quizzes and tests, as well as the visualisation of results through information boards.
- Scalable: Allows specific training content or activities to be adapted based on the needs of stakeholders.

Through the platform, comprehensive support is offered by a navigation map that shows different learning environments that encourage pertinent, well-founded decision-making that is consistent with the expected learning objectives (creating logistical networks, playing freely, conducting a self-assessment through learning paths).

The platform operates as a content aggregator that relies on the following components:

- V-Logistics Editor.

Interactive and flexible environment for users to design their own networks and logistical situations. This tool encourages creativity and the practical application of theoretical knowledge in logistics, allowing users to customise contexts and scenarios according to their learning needs.

It has the following features:

Intuitive interface: Facilitates logistics networking with a user-friendly and easy-to-use user interface.	**E customisation scenarios:** Allows students to design custom logistics scenarios, adjusting variables and parameters to create unique challenges.	**Versatile tools:** Includes a variety of tools and resources to simulate different aspects of logistics, such as transportation, warehousing and inventory management.	**Data visualisation:** Offers advanced visualisation capabilities to help students better understand the structure and operation of logistics networks.

· V-Logistics Simulator (simulation environment)

Environment designed to simulate and execute the logistics networks created in V-Logistics Editor. Its objective is to facilitate the understanding of the interfaces in a logistics network with an interactive experience that allows users to test their designs and strategies and make decisions in real time to address the challenges of logistics management.

V-Logistics Simulator has the following features:

Realistic simulation: Runs logistics networks with a high level of realism, showing how decisions affect the system in real time.	**Interactivity and decision-making:** Allows users to interact with the scenario, make decisions and adjust strategies on the fly.	**Instant feedback:** Immediately shows the impact of the decisions made, allowing for iterative and reflective learning.	**Adaptability to different scenarios:** Able to handle a wide range of designed logistics situations.

V-Logistics makes use of other emerging technologies to improve the learning experience of a wide range of users, from higher education students to professionals in industry, government, civil society or academia. Thus, it can be used in formal education and lifelong learning spaces. In formal education, it complements the traditional curriculum by providing access to additional resources and interactive learning opportunities. For companies and organisations, it is an ideal platform for continuous training and professional development.

When logging in to V-Logistics:

Once logged in to the platform, the user looks at the navigation map, which organises the different sections as follows:

a) Start here: This environment describes the platform as an LCMS resource and manages different sections.

b) Create your logistics network: Here, you can build your own logistics network using V-Logistics Editor. You can create a new game, play a previously created available game or continue a game that was started but not completed.
c) Free Games: This section lists games that can be reviewed and played for free. The conditions of these games are pre-established by each designer.
d) Learning paths: This is the central section of V-Logistics, where the pedagogical intentions of a training path are presented. It includes pre-assessment instruments, didactic sequences and cases that guide the user in what they must do. It also offers a game-generating environment, open educational resources in video format, infographics, cases, manuals, glossary and tools for assessing the development of complex thinking skills, self-regulated learning, gaming experience and user experience. Upon completing all the activities of a learning path, users can request a digital certificate, which is validated by the V-Logistics administration team.
e) Results: in this section, users who completed a learning path can review their results regarding the development of complex thinking, self-regulated learning, gaming experience and user experience skills. The information is presented on information boards.
f) Contact us: This section facilitates different intentions and communication channels between users and the V-Logistics team.
g) Educational Resources: Here, the different resources included in the activities of the V-Logistics platform are categorised (videos, 360° videos, cases, infographics, and didactic sequences among others).
h) Testimonials: this section presents links to representatives of different sectors and the voices of some users.

Analysis of V-Logistics

Some elements that could be incorporated into V-Logistics to enhance its functionality and enrich the learning experience:

1. Incident and Contingency Simulation
   - Description: Incorporate random or scheduled events, such as natural disasters, strikes, supply chain disruptions, or fluctuations in input prices.
   - Benefit: These events would help students develop risk management skills and make decisions in crisis situations, preparing them to face uncertainty in real-world environments.
2. Sustainability and Carbon Footprint Analysis
   - Description: Add modules to calculate the environmental impact of logistics decisions, such as energy consumption, CO_2 emissions, and waste.

- Benefit: This would facilitate the teaching of sustainable logistics and commitment to responsible practices, aligning with Sustainable Development Goals (SDGs) and raising students' awareness of the importance of minimising environmental impact.

3. Artificial Intelligence for Demand Prediction and Optimisation
   - Description: Integrate AI algorithms to predict demand and optimise inventory, production, and distribution decisions based on historical patterns and demand trends.
   - Benefit: Students could see how AI supports decision-making and learn to apply advanced technology in the supply chain, developing skills to interpret and adjust algorithm recommendations.
4. Finance and Budget Integration
   - Description: Add a financial component that allows users to see the impact of their logistics decisions on operating costs, profit margins, and return on investment.
   - Benefit: This function would enable students to understand the relationship between logistics decisions and the company's financial performance, promoting a comprehensive perspective on business management.
5. Customisation of Roles and Responsibilities in Teams
   - Description: Implement the possibility for students to assume specific roles (e.g. inventory manager, transport leader, purchasing analyst) and coordinate their actions to achieve team objectives.
   - Benefit: This would facilitate the development of teamwork and communication skills, as well as an understanding of how different roles relate to and affect each other in a supply chain.
6. Decision-Making Based on Key Performance Indicators (KPI) Module
   - Description: Include a section that allows users to develop, monitor, and interpret key performance indicators (KPIs) in real time, such as cycle time, service level, or order fulfilment rate.
   - Benefit: Students could practice data-driven management by continuously evaluating supply chain performance and making informed decisions.
7. International Trade and Customs Legislation Simulation
   - Description: Incorporate scenarios that include aspects of international trade, such as tariffs, customs clearance times, and import/export regulations.
   - Benefit: This will enable students to understand the complexities of global trade and how tariff barriers and regulatory policies can affect product flow.
8. Gamification and Immediate Feedback
   - Description: Add gamification elements, such as achievements, levels, and rewards, along with immediate feedback on decisions made.

- Benefit: This would increase student motivation and engagement, providing incentives to continuously improve and learn interactively from mistakes.

9. Advanced Visualisation of Flows and Logistics Maps
   - Description: Develop dynamic visualisations of logistics flows on an interactive map, with real-time tracking options for shipments, inventories, and transport routes.
   - Benefit: This would facilitate logistics network analysis and help students better understand the spatial impact of their decisions, aiding in route optimisation and resource distribution.
10. Negotiation Scenarios with Suppliers and Customers
    - Description: Include negotiation options that allow students to interact with suppliers and customers, adjusting delivery terms, prices, and service levels.
    - Benefit: This would help develop negotiation and effective communication skills, essential for managing supply chain relationships.
11. Augmented Reality (AR) Integration
    - Description: Use AR to visualise and manipulate supply chain elements, such as inventories and material flow, in a three-dimensional environment.
    - Benefit: This would provide an immersive experience that helps students visualise complex logistics processes, improving spatial understanding and analysis of supply chain layout.

Comparison of V-Logistics with Similar Platforms

1. Realistic Simulation of Logistics Environments
   - V-Logistics: Specifically designed to provide a realistic experience by integrating key areas of a company (suppliers, factories, distribution centres, stores, wholesale customers), allowing students to experience a complete logistics flow and understand the interdependence between areas.
   - The Beer Game: Although a popular game for teaching basic supply chain concepts and the bullwhip effect, it focuses more on information flow and inventory management in a simple four-actor chain. It does not allow scenario customisation or integration of multiple functional areas like V-Logistics.
   - MIT Supply Chain Simulator (SCM Globe): Allows students to design and operate supply chain networks in global scenarios, but it generally focuses on strategic planning rather than interaction among specific operational areas.
2. Customisation and Adaptability of Scenarios
   - V-Logistics: Allows the creation of customised scenarios, where users can choose the type of business, define the number of suppliers, factories, and distribution centres, facilitating a learning experience tailored to different contexts and study objectives.

- Logistics Simulator (LLamasoft): Offers advanced simulation of supply chain networks but is more geared toward data analysis and large network optimisation, with less focus on step-by-step teaching or direct student interaction in scenario setup.
- SAP ERPsim: Simulates business management in an ERP environment, where students make decisions about sales, production, and inventory. However, its scenario customisation level is more limited and requires prior ERP knowledge to fully benefit from the experience.

3. Emphasis on Experiential and Adaptive Learning
   - V-Logistics: Promotes 'learning by doing', allowing students to adapt to market changes, demand adjustments, and supply chain problems, fostering decision-making skills in complex situations.
   - Inchainge's The Fresh Connection: Allows students to make decisions in a supply chain environment, especially in the food industry, where they experience the consequences of their decisions in an integrated chain. However, its adaptability to other sectors is limited, focusing mainly on inventory and purchasing management.
   - Business on the Move: An educational board game that teaches basic logistics concepts, aimed at initial educational levels. It lacks the adaptability and scenario depth of V-Logistics, though it is effective for introducing students to basic logistics and transportation concepts.
4. Integration of Operational and Strategic Variables
   - V-Logistics: Provides a comprehensive perspective by integrating operational decisions, such as supplier selection and warehouse management, with strategic aspects like distribution network expansion or product diversification, offering a complete business view.
   - Littlefield Technologies: A simulator that allows students to manage a production plant, optimising resources in a manufacturing setting. Although it provides a detailed view of production, it does not cover the entire supply chain or integrate diverse functional areas like V-Logistics.
5. Development of Customised Indicators
   - V-Logistics: Encourages students to develop and interpret specific logistics indicators, facilitating data analysis practice and the creation of custom metrics to evaluate the performance of their supply chains.
   - Simulators like SCM Globe and LLamasoft: Offer data analysis tools and predefined indicators, but customisation for creating new indicators is limited and typically requires advanced technical expertise.

Characteristic	V-Logistics	The Beer Game	SCM Globe	SAP ERPsim	The Fresh Connection	Business on the Move	Littlefield Technologies
Realism of the logistics environment	High	Medium	Medium-High	High	High	Low	Medium
Scenario customisation	High	Low	Medium	Medium	Low	Low	Medium
Focus on experiential learning	High	Medium	Medium	Medium	High	Low	Medium
Integration of functional areas	Complete	Limited	Partial	Partial	Partial	Limited	Production-focused
Customised indicators	High	No	Limited	Limited	Limited	No	Limited

WHAT DO THE STUDIES SAY? …

On the Proposal Made by the Innovation Project

The implementation of logistical simulations and game-based learning (GBL) in education has been shown to have a significant impact on the development of critical skills and essential competencies in students (Kokkalia, 2017; Zhonggen, 2019). Using simulation platforms, students can face complex and dynamic scenarios that replicate real-world situations, thus promoting critical thinking and informed decision-making. These tools not only improve the understanding of logistics processes and supply chain management but also encourage self-management and autonomy in learning. Studies have revealed that students who participate in logistics simulations develop a greater openness to new learning opportunities, initiative, independence in the educational process and a more robust perception of themselves as effective learners (Pacheco-Velázquez, 2022; Olexová & Gajdoš, 2016). This approach, based on gamification and active learning, results in a more interactive and immersive educational experience, which better prepares students for the challenges of the contemporary labour market.

In addition, logistic simulations have been shown to be particularly effective in strengthening self-directed learning (SDL) skills (Pacheco-Velázquez, 2020). Through the use of simulations, students not only acquire technical knowledge but also develop transversal competencies, such as the ability to analyse and solve complex problems, time management and the ability to work collaboratively. These simulated learning environments provide a safe space to experiment and learn from mistakes, which is crucial for the development of resilience and adaptability. Studies have shown that participants in logistic simulations report a significant increase in their love of learning and their intrinsic motivation to explore and understand new concepts (Pacheco-Velázquez, et al., 2023). In addition, research underscores that simulations and serious games are effective tools for teaching complex skills and advanced techniques, which are crucial to Industry 4.0. In summary, logistics simulations not only improve academic performance and understanding of specific content but also equip students with the necessary tools for continuous and autonomous learning, preparing them to face the complexity and demands of modern industry.

References

Kokkalia, G., Drigas, A., Economou, A., Roussos, P., & Choli, S. (2017). The use of serious games in preschool education. *International Journal of Emerging Technologies in Learning*, *12*(11). https://doi.org/10.3991/ijet.v12i11.6991.

Zhonggen, Y. (2019). A meta-analysis of use of serious games in education over a decade. *International Journal of Computer Games Technology*, *2019*(1), 4797032. https://doi.org/10.1155/2019/4797032.

Pacheco-Velázquez, E. (2022). Effects of the use of simulators and an online platform in logistics education. *International Journal on Interactive Design and Manufacturing (IJIDeM) 16*(2), 439–457.

Olexová, C., & Gajdoš, J. (2016). Logistics simulation game proposal–A tool for employees' induction. Quality Innovation Prosperity, 20(2), 53–68.

Pacheco-Velázquez, E. (2020, March). Using gamification to develop self-directed learning. In *Proceedings of the 2020 International Conference on Education Development and Studies* (pp. 1–5).

Pacheco-Velázquez, E., Salinas-Navarro, D. E., & Ramírez-Montoya, M. S. (2023). Serious Games and Experiential Learning: Options for Engineering Education. *International Journal of Serious Games, 10*(3), 3–21.

WE INVITE YOU TO REFLECT ...

We invite you to reflect on the impacts and benefits of logistics simulation in game-based learning. Consider the following questions to deepen the educational innovation proposal presented:

1. In what ways do you think the use of logistics simulations can transform traditional teaching in your area of study or work?

---

2. How can simulations and game-based learning foster the development of self-management, complex thinking and self-directed learning skills in each student? *It considers the implications of enabling students to manage their own learning processes and how this can influence their ability to adapt to changing and complex work contexts.*

---

3. What challenges might arise when implementing logistics simulations in an educational setting, and how can they be overcome? *It recognises and analyses potential technological, pedagogical or institutional barriers that might arise and suggests strategies to address these obstacles and maximise positive impact.*

Impacts and Benefits of Logistics Simulation and Game-Based Learning in Education

Is It Possible to Transform Traditional Teaching with Logistical Simulations?

The use of logistics simulations can revolutionise traditional teaching in several areas of study, especially those related to logistics, trade, and supply chain management. These tools allow students to interact with realistic and dynamic scenarios, promoting a deeper understanding of theoretical concepts. Through simulation, students can experience the consequences of their decisions in a controlled environment, facilitating hands-on learning and knowledge retention.

Compared to conventional educational methods, where teaching is mainly theoretical and expository, logistics simulations offer an immersive and participatory experience. The integration of these tools can change the dynamics of learning through the following ways:

- The students cease to be **passive receivers** of information and become active participants who make decisions and solve problems.
- The practical application of theoretical concepts in simulated situations helps consolidate learning.
- Simulations require each student **to analyse data, evaluate alternatives and make informed decisions.**
- Many logistics simulations are developed in teams, promoting **joint work and the exchange of ideas.**

How Can Skills Be Developed Through Simulations and Game-Based Learning?

Simulations and game-based learning can significantly foster the development of key skills such as self-management, complex thinking and self-directed learning.

By enabling students to manage their own learning process, these tools achieve the following:

- **Promote self-management:** Each student learns to plan, organise and evaluate their actions within the simulation, developing time and resource management skills.
- **Encourage complex thinking:** Simulations present multifaceted problems that require the analysis of multiple variables and the consideration of diverse perspectives, which stimulates systems thinking and complex problem solving.
- **Drive self-directed learning:** Each student must actively seek out information, try different approaches and learn from their mistakes, which teaches them to be self-taught and adapt to new challenges.

These skills are crucial for the modern social context, where adaptability and the ability to manage changing and complex environments is highly valued.

What are the Challenges and Strategies in the Implementation of Logistics Simulations in Education?

Implementing logistics simulations in an educational environment presents several challenges, including the following:

- Lack of access to appropriate technology, such as computers and specialised software.
- Teachers may be reluctant to adopt new methodologies due to a lack of familiarity or the perception that they are complicated to implement.
- Resources need to be used to conduct continuous training and create communities.
- Budgetary constraints and curricular rigidity can make it difficult to integrate new educational tools. To address this, it is critical that institutions seek external funding, such as grants, and work on making curricula more flexible.

Maximising the positive impact of logistics simulations in education requires a comprehensive approach that combines investment in technology, teacher training, institutional flexibility and innovative assessment methods. By addressing these challenges, simulations can profoundly transform learning and prepare students to successfully meet the challenges of the modern world of work.

SDGs in Education

Strengthening the SDGs: V-Logistic's Contribution

V-Logistics' goals are aligned with SDG 4, which focuses on ensuring quality, inclusive and equitable education. At V-Logistics, we work to improve the quality and efficiency of the development of these capabilities.

In addition, V-Logistics aims to improve management and decision-making skills, which contributes to sustainable economic growth and the creation of decent jobs. This is directly related to SDG 8, which sets targets for decent work and sustained, inclusive and sustainable economic growth, with full and productive employment for all.

Figure 4. SDGs mobilised through the S4L platform

V-Logistics also acts as a tool to define companies' logistics operations, linking to SDG 9, which focuses on industry, innovation and infrastructure (Figure 4). This goal seeks to build resilient infrastructure, promote inclusive and sustainable industrialisation and foster innovation.

TO KNOW MORE …

The Link between the SDGs and the Proposal

Sustainable Development Goals Report 2020

Authors: UN

Reference: UN (2020). Sustainable Development Goals Report 2020.https://www.un.org/sustainabledevelopment/es/progress-report/

▶ We invite you to explore an essential study on the 2030 Agenda for Sustainable Development, a global plan launched in 2015 with the ambitious goal of eradicating poverty and promoting peace, prosperity and opportunity for all on a healthy planet. With its seventeen Sustainable Development Goals (SDGs), this agenda calls for profound transformations in our financial, economic and political systems to guarantee universal human rights. While we have seen progress, such as reduced school dropout rates and improvements in access to clean water, the COVID-19 pandemic has widened existing inequalities, disproportionately affecting the most vulnerable and slowing progress towards these goals. This report calls for a coordinated international response that strengthens health systems, ensures universal access to treatments and vaccines and promotes a sustainable and equitable economic recovery.

Industry, Innovation, and Infrastructure Report 2021

Authors: UN

Reference: UN (2021). Industry, Innovation, and Infrastructure Report 2021. United Nations Department of Economic and Social Affairs https://www.un.org/development/desa/dpad/publication/world-economic-situation-and-prospects-2021/

▶ Discover an essential study published by the United Nations Department of Economic and Social Affairs that can help you learn more about this topic. This report examines progress and challenges related to SDG 9, which focuses on building resilient infrastructure, promoting inclusive and sustainable industrialisation and fostering innovation. These elements are key to achieving the goals of the 2030 Agenda. By understanding and supporting these pillars, we can contribute to building a stronger and more equitable world for all.

World Employment and Social Outlook – Trends 2021

Authors: International Labour Organization

Reference: International Labour Organization (2021). World Employment and Social Outlook – Trends 2021. https://www.oitcinterfor.org/en/node/8150

▶ Today I want to invite you to explore a crucial report published by the International Labour Organization (ILO). This study analyses global trends and challenges in employment and working conditions, focusing on the impact of the COVID-19 pandemic on decent work and economic growth. Through detailed data and analysis, the report shows us how countries can recover and make progress towards SDG 8, which promotes decent work and sustainable economic growth.

New Educational Scenarios

EDUCATIONAL SCENARIO aimed at students

Logistics Simulation Workshop with V-Logistics in the Company

Linked SDGs

Activity

The activity consists of an interactive workshop designed for students who will take on the role of employees of an international trade company. In this role, they will make use of the V-Logistics platform, which will allow them to simulate international trade scenarios and customs operations. The activity has a playful and participatory approach to promote learning and team cohesion.

Objective

To improve the logistics skills and decision-making of each participant, providing a practical understanding of the impact of logistics on international trade and customs operations.

Beginning

1. Initial preparations
   - Technical configuration and testing of the V-Logistics platform on the computer equipment to be used.
   - Distribution of support materials to each participant (manuals, guides, etc.).
2. Workshop introduction
   - Presentation of the facilitating team and objectives of the workshop.
   - Explanation of the dynamics of the workshop and the importance of logistics simulations.
   - Brief introduction to the V-Logistics platform and its functionalities.

Development

1. Phase One – Introduction to Simulation
   - Detailed explanation of the platform and its tools.
   - Assignment of roles and tasks within the simulated environment, encouraging teamwork.
2. Phase Two – Execution of the simulation
   - Participants interact with the platform to manage logistics and customs operations.
   - Problem solving and decision-making in real time, facing simulated scenarios.
   - Incorporation of playful elements, such as challenges and prizes, to motivate active participation.
3. Phase Three – Evaluation and adjustments
   - Monitoring of the decisions and performance of each participant.
   - Making adjustments and corrections based on instant feedback from the platform.

Closing

1. Analysis and discussion
   - Discussion and reflection session on the decisions made during the simulation.
   - Evaluation of the results and comparison with real scenarios.
2. Feedback and conclusions
   - Compilation of opinions and suggestions from each participant.
   - Summary of key learnings and formal closing of the workshop.

Evaluation

- User experience (UX) and eGame Flow questionnaires (which are integrated into the V-Logistics platform).
- Evaluation of practical skills through direct observation and feedback from facilitators.
- Analysis of decisions made and their impact on the simulation.

Evidence of Learning

- Results of the UX and eGame Flow questionnaires.
- Individual and group performance reports on the platform.
- Recording of decisions and their consequences within the simulation.

Materials Needed

- Access to computers with internet connection.
- V-Logistics platform installed and configured.
- Support materials (manuals, guides, presentations).
- UX, eGame Flow and eComplexity instrument (Castillo-Martínez & Ramírez-Montoya, 2022).

Reference

Castillo-Martínez, I. M. & Ramírez-Montoya, M. S. (2022). Instrumento eComplexity: Medición de la percepción de estudiantes de educación superior acerca de su competencia de razonamiento para la complejidad. https://hdl.handle.net/11285/643622

EDUCATIONAL SCENARIO aimed at teachers

Action Lab for Learning in Simulations

Linked SDGs

4 QUALITY EDUCATION

Activity

Use of V-Logistics (open educational platform that uses simulations and serious games) to encourage the development of complex thinking competence and encourage self-regulated learning through problem solving and decision-making.

Objective

To create a logistics network for an enterprise in which participants will make decisions in safe scenarios.

Beginning

Teachers will offer a brief introduction to the V-Logistics platform, highlighting the objectives of the laboratory activity. An explanation on how to navigate the platform and how to use the simulations and resources available will be provided by the facilitator.

Development

Participants will explore simulations that replicate complex business and logistics environments. In these safe scenarios, they will be able to practise decision-making, with the aim of creating a logistical network for an open education project. In addition, access to open educational resources, such as educational videos, informative articles and quizzes, will be facilitated to deepen the concepts of self-regulated learning and reasoning for complexity. This activity will also promote learning from diverse perspectives and the integration of knowledge of business, logistics and open education, thus offering a multidisciplinary approach.

Closing

A closing session where each participant shares their experiences and learnings will be held. Faculty will provide feedback, and thoughtful discussion about skills acquired will be encouraged.

Evaluation

The evaluation process can be established through feedback surveys distributed to the participants, the observations of the facilitators and the ventures developed.

The platform has tools that will allow you to assess the level of perception of complex thinking, self-directed learning, user experience (UX) and game flow (eGame Flow) once the use of V-Logistics has been experienced.

The eComplexity instrument (Castillo-Martínez & Ramírez-Montoya, 2022) is administered twice: as a pre-test and a post-test applied after the learning experience. The questionnaire uses a Likert scale for self-assessment of the level of complex thinking mastery in four dimensions: complex, systemic, critical and innovative thinking. In addition, the eComplexity instrument measures knowledge, skills and values. Similarly, UX and eGame Flow instruments are administered to measure user experience and gaming experience, respectively. In addition, a self-directed learning instrument (pre-test and post-test) is used, with a scale to evaluate the organisation, management and solution of problems in learning.

Evidence of Learning

As evidence of learning, the ventures proposed and developed by the participants will be considered. These will allow the understanding and application of the knowledge acquired to be visualised.

Digital Materials or Tools

- S4L simulation platform
- Open educational resources (videos, articles, quizzes)
- Online collaboration tools (e.g. Zoom, Microsoft Teams)

Reference

Castillo-Martínez, I. M. & Ramírez-Montoya, M. S. (2022). Instrumento eComplexity: Medición de la percepción de estudiantes de educación superior acerca de su competencia de razonamiento para la complejidad. https://hdl.handle.net/11285/643622

EDUCATIONAL SCENARIO aimed at companies

Business Workshop for the Development of Logistics Concepts

Linked SDGs

8 DECENT WORK AND ECONOMIC GROWTH

Activity

Participants will develop skills to design and optimise logistics networks through simulations and educational games. This activity uses simulations to teach about complex logistics systems and processes, encouraging critical and creative thinking.

Objective

To develop the capacity of each participant to think critically and creatively about complex problems, as well as to learn to identify and apply appropriate solutions through the characterisation of different logistics facilities, such as warehouses, distribution centres and transport terminals.

Beginning

Participants will meet in a virtual environment where they will receive an introduction to the key concepts of logistics and the use of simulations as learning tools. A brief introduction is given on the importance of V-Logistics in terms of the flexibility and ease of recreating different logistics scenarios.

Development

1. Enter the page.
2. Read the case study on Gaermont Sports, available at https://medium.com/@ernesto1411/gaermont-sport-da9a1660b9c4.
3. Participants will work in groups to solve logistical problems, encouraging collaboration and the development of soft skills. They will perform the exercises specified in the case study.

Closing

Each group will present their solutions to the logistical problems and receive feedback from the facilitators. A discussion will be held to consolidate learning and reflect on experiences.

Evaluation

Based on what was recognised in the Gaermont Sports case study, participants in the business area are asked to write and develop a case based on the characteristics of their own company.

Tests that are incorporated into the platform before and after the activity will be used to measure learning, along with satisfaction surveys, facilitators' observations and case studies developed by each participant. The following instruments are incorporated into the platform: eComplexity (Castillo-Martínez & Ramírez-Montoya, 2022), self-directed learning, user experience and eGame Flow.

Evidence of Learning

The design of your company's logistics chain must be represented in the simulation. The scenario developed must correspond to the narrative of each participant about the case they have developed.

Digital Materials or Tools

Online communication and collaboration tools (e.g. Zoom, Microsoft Teams)

Videos on using the game editor or game creator

- https://youtu.be/kPb3qPUIwuo
- https://youtu.be/1cP8yY_mZx0
- https://youtu.be/BuRBUQCh8gA
- https://youtu.be/cHoFPU9Gxzk
- https://youtu.be/TQLb-dMLDIw
- https://youtu.be/G280SI5Xrrs
- https://youtu.be/10qFkKKy0wU

Videos on using the simulator

- https://youtu.be/RCGIdSLcWTw
- https://youtu.be/gaNNQ5GZifo
- https://youtu.be/Z0Qe449BLMI
- https://youtu.be/qWselY_rzl0
- https://youtu.be/IPJoPd30NhQ

Reference

Castillo-Martínez, I. M. & Ramírez-Montoya, M. S. (2022). Instrumento eComplexity: Medición de la percepción de estudiantes de educación superior acerca de su competencia de razonamiento para la complejidad. https://hdl.handle.net/11285/643622

EDUCATIONAL SCENARIO aimed at NGOs

Practical Logistics Simulation Workshop with V-Logistics for Women Entrepreneurs

Linked SDGs

Activity

This dynamic workshop immerses the women of the group of logistics management through the V-Logistics platform. Through practical simulations, they strengthen their entrepreneurial and strategic skills, preparing them to develop leadership skills in a globalised and equitable business environment.

Objective

To develop competencies for women in the group concerning practical aspects of logistics, facilitating their integration into and effective leadership in the business world.

Beginning

1. Preparation and welcome
   - Initial configuration of the V-Logistics platform for an interactive and educational experience.
   - Presentation of the facilitating team, highlighting the strategic relevance of logistics in business development and the importance of female participation.
2. Workshop introduction
   - Initial session on the importance of logistics in business competitiveness and opportunities for women entrepreneurs.

   Example of a real-world application

   Imagine Lucía, an entrepreneur who wants to expand her business of artisanal products to international markets. Using V-Logistics, Lucía learns how to optimise her shipping and distribution processes, reducing costs and delivery times.

Development

1. Hands-on training
   - Guided instruction on the use of V-Logistics, exploring key functions for supply chain management and logistics.
   - Practical examples of business applications with a focus on real logistics challenges.

   Example of a real-world application

   Maria, another workshop participant, runs a small health food business. Through simulations, she learns how to effectively manage the supply chain from production to the end customer, improving the quality of service and the satisfaction of her customers.

Development *(continued)*

2. Business simulation
   - Implementation of logistics simulations to solve problems such as efficient distribution, inventory management and route optimisation.
   - Teamwork to make strategic decisions and face dynamic scenarios.

   Example of a real-world application

   Ana, who leads a collective of women producers of local handicrafts, uses simulations to coordinate export logistics to new markets, ensuring the timely arrival of their products and complying with international quality standards.
3. Analysis and reflection
   - Post-simulation review session to discuss adopted strategies, share key learnings and explore practical applications in real business.
   - Discussion on the importance of logistics in business success and the ability of women to lead in this field.

Closing

1. Conclusions and next steps
   - Recap of individual and group achievements during the workshop.
   - Focus on continuing personal and professional development in logistics and business strategy.

   Example of a real-world application

   After the workshop, participants such as Lucia, Maria and Ana implement the strategies learned in their businesses, observing significant improvements in operational efficiency and competitiveness in the global market.
2. Impact and follow-up
   - Evaluation of the impact of the workshop on the logistical and strategic skills of the participants.
   - Recommendations for future business development activities and programmes within the group, strengthening female inclusion and leadership in strategic sectors.

Evaluation

- Use of tailored user experience (UX) questionnaires to measure the platform performance effectiveness and satisfaction with V-Logistics.
- Evaluation of strategic decisions made during simulations through qualitative and quantitative feedback.
- Analysis of the development of entrepreneurial and strategic skills as evidence of learning.

Materials Needed

- Access to computers with internet connection and V-Logistics configuration.
- How-to guides and digital resources on business logistics and strategy.

EDUCATIONAL SCENARIO aimed at lifelong learning

Practical Gamification and Serious Games Workshop: Lifelong Learning with V-Logistics

Linked SDGs

Activity

Workshop that uses the V-Logistics platform to introduce participants to the world of logistics through serious games and gamification. It focuses on the development of key competencies for continuous learning and professional growth.

Objective

To promote active and continuous learning through serious games and gamification, using V-Logistics as the main tool for the simulation and management of logistics chains.

Beginning

1. Welcome and introduction
   - Introduction to the concept of serious games and gamification in lifelong learning.
   - Importance of logistics in the global economy and professional development.

   Example of a real-world application

   Imagine Carlos, a growing professional who wants to improve his logistics skills to meet his career goals. Through serious games on the V-Logistics platform, Carlos learns how to optimise distribution routes and improve the operational efficiency of his company.

Development

1. Hands-on training
   - Guided use of V-Logistics to simulate real logistics management situations.
   - Practical business application examples focused on global logistics challenges.

   Example of a real-world application example

   Maria, an entrepreneur who manages a local supply chain, uses simulations to learn inventory management and cost optimisation strategies, thus improving the competitiveness of her business in today's market.
2. Business simulation
   - Implementation of dynamic scenarios to solve complex logistics problems.
   - Teamwork to make strategic decisions and face emerging challenges.

   Example of a real-world application

   Ana, a trainee working with a local NGO, uses V-Logistics to coordinate the distribution of resources to remote communities, improving the efficiency and impact of humanitarian interventions.

Development *(continued)*

3. Analysis and reflection
    - Post-simulation review session to discuss effective strategies and share meaningful learnings.
    - Discussion about the application of serious games in educational and professional environments.

Closing

1. Conclusions and next steps
    - Evaluation of individual and group achievements during the workshop.
    - Focus on the continuous application of skills acquired in professional and educational practice.

   Example of a real-world application

   After the workshop, participants such as Carlos, María and Ana apply the strategies learned in their respective fields, observing tangible improvements in operational efficiency and strategic decision-making.
2. Impact and follow-up
    - Evaluation of the impact of serious games on learning and professional development.
    - Recommendations for future lifelong learning and gamified education initiatives.

Evaluation

- Use of adapted assessment tools to measure effectiveness and learning through serious play.
- Assessment of competencies developed as evidence of learning and career progression.

Digital Materials or Tools

- Access to the V-Logistics platform and complementary educational resources.
- 360° videos, infographics and how-to guides to facilitate continuous and autonomous learning.
- Support materials and documentation to reinforce concepts learned during the workshop.

The hands-on gamification workshop and serious games on the V-Logistics platform strengthen the logistics competencies of each participant while promotes lifelong learning dynamically and effectively. Through interactive simulations and collaborative work, professionals and students can develop essential skills to face the current challenges of the global market. Continuing these initiatives not only improves education and professional development, but also contributes to the fulfilment of the SDGs, promoting inclusive, equitable and quality education for all people.

Recommendations for Implementation

The implementation of the V-Logistics platform must be adapted to individual stakeholders' contexts. The four key sectors and the specific benefits for each of them are identified below (Figure 5).

Recommendations for implementing the S4L platform.

- **Academia:** Fosters metacognitive competencies and complex thinking through serious games and simulations.
- **Small and Medium Enterprises (SMEs) Industry :** Tackle management, knowledge and technology challenges with the V-Logistics logistics simulator.
- **Government agencies:** Drives resilience and sustainable growth in the face of Industry 5.0 challenges, improving relevant skills.
- **Civil Society:** promotes continuous learning and connection between sectors to meet the needs of Industry 5.0.

The V-Logistics platform offers a navigation map with three sections of main activities, all supported by the logistics editor and simulator:

a) Build your logistics network
b) Free Games
c) Learning paths

In addition, there are complementary sections to access the scoreboard, contact the team, access educational resources and read testimonials of use.

Consider the objectives of each section of the platform:

- **Build your logistics network:** Provide each participant with an integrated editor and simulator to apply and experiment with logistics principles, decisions and strategies in a controlled but dynamic environment.

- **Free games:** Share a variety of previously created logistical games, with the intention of enriching the practical experience of each user in a fun way and at no cost. These games facilitate interactive and applied learning of topics in logistics, operations and supply chains, promoting the development of competencies through experimentation.

- **Learning paths:** Guide the participant through a structured didactic sequence. It begins with the initial self-perception of competencies such as complex thinking and self-regulated learning and progresses through cases and logistical simulation exercises that allow the development of these competencies to be assessed. The game experience and the user experience are also assessed, corroborating the development of skills at the end of the activity through specific instruments.

Preparation and Welcome

To ensure the success of the implementation, it is key to share a welcome kit with each participant in advance that includes the following:

- Invitation to the activity.
. Registration on the platform.
- Objectives and intentions.
- Agenda.
- Signing of informed consent.
- Accompaniment by a facilitator, either in the room or in a virtual environment.

In addition, it is important to set the scope and achievement expectations for each scheduled experience. The learning paths section is the only one that allows you to display a results dashboard and issue digital certificates of participation in an automated way.

Figure 5. Recommendations for implementing the S4L platform

Considering User Experience

As an example of user experience and platform effectiveness validation, a pilot study was conducted with 249 students from eight universities across five Latin American countries to assess the usability of this simulation generator on logistics education. The study revealed significant findings: (a) the simulation generator provides learners with flexible and tailored educational experiences. (b) the Interface and Performance and Effectiveness aspects of the Virtual Logistics were highly rated, achieving a 'Good to Excellent' usability level:

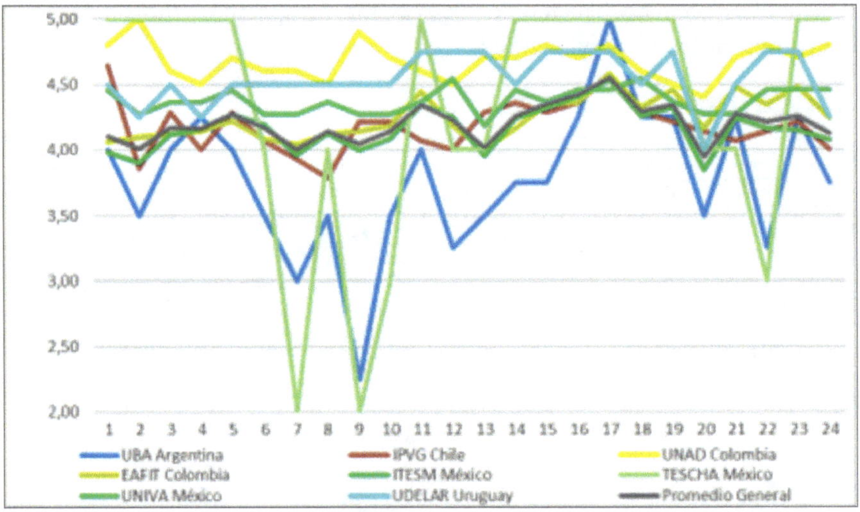

General Usability Report

Dimension	Merits	Usability Level
Content Organisation	78,80 %	Good
Navigation	78,83 %	Good
Interface	82,98 %	Excellent
Performance and Effectiveness	80,30 %	Excellent

These results demonstrate student's satisfaction, and therefore, the transformative potential of simulation-based learning tools in logistics education. Virtual Logistics offers valuable guidance for educators, policymakers, and industry leaders, aligning educational tools with dynamic requirements, ensuring that future professionals are well-equipped to face the complexities of the modern logistics landscape.

As an example of the application in research studies, the serious game was applied to students in the business field, as well as to students in industrial engineering and production engineering programmes (n = 212, range of evaluation: 0–7, being 7 excellence).

Description of Evaluated Factors, Means, and Standard Deviations

Factor	Mean	Standard Deviation
Concentration (C)	5.67	1.15
Goal Clarity (G)	5.98	1.21
Feedback (F)	5.45	1.39
Challenge (H)	5.76	1.13
Autonomy (A)	6.00	0.91
Immersion (I)	5.44	1.52
Social Interaction (S)	5.54	1.35

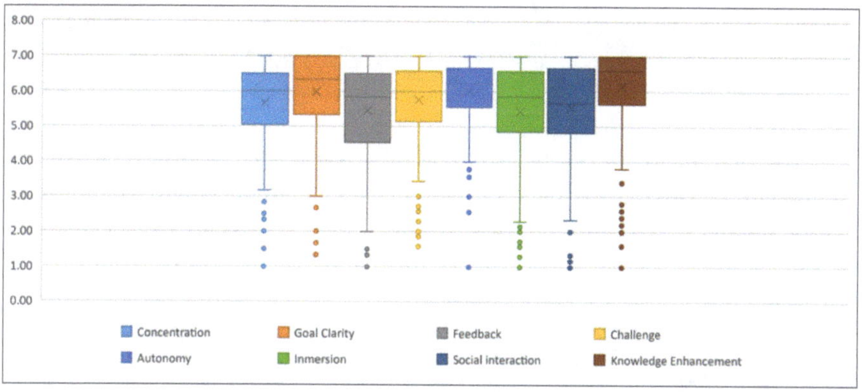

Implementation

Success Case Report in Colombia

On Monday, 30 September 2024, Dr Ernesto Pacheco from Tecnológico de Monterrey implemented V-Logistics in collaboration with partners from the National Open and Distance University (UNAD) and Antonio Nariño University (UAN). These institutions are currently interested in incorporating the simulator into the academic programme of two courses that are currently being redesigned.

They partnered with a working group called Logyca, which aims to add value to companies for their growth and development through data analysis and information quality, generating applicable knowledge in value chain management. A tour of the company was conducted to understand the logistics chain.

logyca

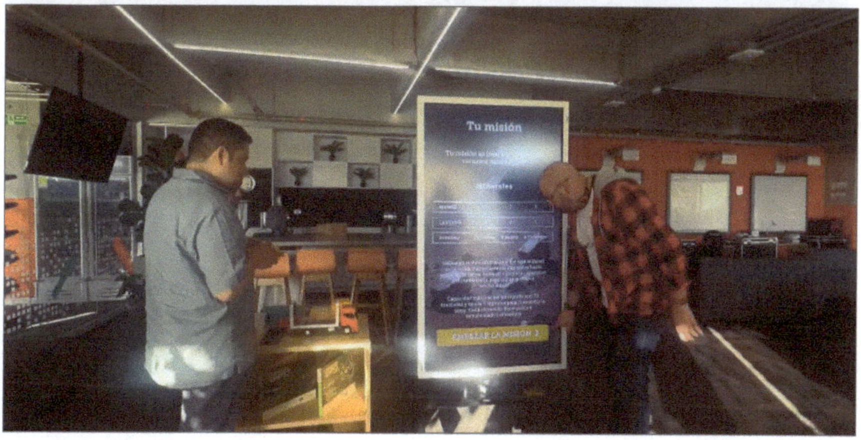
Tu misión

Validating the effectiveness of the V-Logistics platform is essential to ensure that this educational tool fulfils its purpose of providing a practical, immersive learning experience aligned with the real demands of the logistics sector. Evaluating its impact in different academic and professional contexts not only enables improvements in its functionality and content but also strengthens its relevance and applicability in developing key skills such as decision-making, problem solving, and critical thinking. By validating its effectiveness, the value of V-Logistics is confirmed as an essential resource in logistics education, preparing students and professionals to successfully meet the challenges of today's work environment.

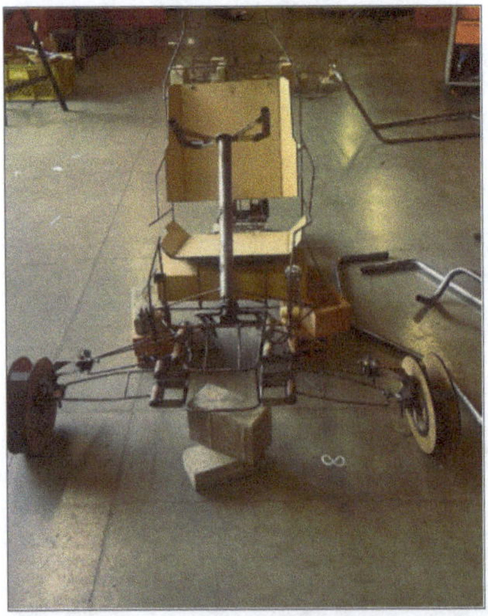

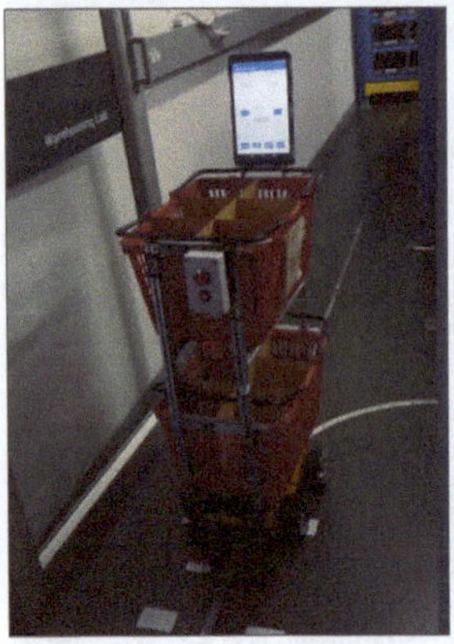

OPEN EDUCATIONAL RESOURCES (OER)

OER: V-Logistics Session 1. Introduction. Login
Author: Ernesto Armando Pacheco-Velázquez
Reference: Pacheco-Velázquez, E. A. (2024). V-Logistics Session 1. Introduction. Login [Infographic]. https://repositorio.tec.mx/handle/11285/652417

▶ We start with an educational infographic that will help you get started on the right foot in your V-Logistics course. This infographic guides you step by step on how to log in, giving you clear and straightforward visual support for the first session of the course. Imagine that we are together, unravelling every detail so that your start is simple and hassle-free. This visual tool is perfect for making sure you get the most out of all that V-Logistics has to offer. Join this learning experience, and let's make your educational journey smooth and successful together. Let's start a great learning adventure!

OER: V-Logistics – Virtual Platform for Logistics Learning
Author: Leonardo David Glasserman Morales
Reference: Glasserman Morales, L. D. (2024). V-Logistics—Virtual platform for logistics learning [Video]. https://hdl.handle.net/11285/676168

▶ We invite you to explore an educational video resource that presents V-Logistics, a learning-content management system (LCMS) that promotes complex thinking and self-regulated learning competencies. This system is based on the advances of Industry 5.0, integrating artificial intelligence, simulation, data analysis and open educational resources, and aims to train professionals who are capable of achieving meaningful and continuous learning throughout their lives. Imagine that we are together, exploring how V-Logistics can revolutionise the way we learn and teach, preparing students to face the challenges of the future with critical and adaptive skills. Join this learning community, and let's discover the potential of this innovative tool together. Let's learn and grow together!

OER: Playing and Learning: Developing Life Skills
Authors: Carolina Alcántar (interviewer), Azeneth Patiño and Leonardo Glasserman (interviewed)
Reference: Carolina Alcántar, C., Patiño, A. & Glasserman Morales, L. D. (2024). Playing and learning: developing life skills [Video]. Webcast program: Future of education in complexity. Tecnológico de Monterrey. https://hdl.handle.net/11285/676178

▶ We share with you an educational resource, in interview format, entitled 'Playing and learning: development of skills for life'. In this fascinating webinar, Carolina Alcántar interviews specialists Azeneth Patiño and Leonardo Glasserman, who share with us how serious games can be powerful tools for the development of life skills. Imagine that we are all in this conversation together, discovering how these resources can improve complex thinking, decision-making, problem solving and time management. Join us on this exploration, and let's see how play can become an effective educational strategy. Let's learn from this great interview!

OER: Analysing the Advantages of Using Simulators in Logistics Education
Authors: Pamela Olivo (interviewer), Iván Andrés Arana González and Ricardo Thierry (interviewees)
Reference: Olivo, P., Arana González, I. A. & Thierry, R. (2024). Analyzing the advantages of the use of simulators in logistics education [Video]. Webcast program: Future of education in complexity. Tecnológico de Monterrey. https://hdl.handle.net/11285/676179

▶ Through this fascinating educational webinar organised by the S4L project entitled 'Analyzing the advantages of the use of simulators in logistics education', you will have the opportunity to discover how these tools can revolutionise learning in the field of supply chains. Imagine that we are together listening to Pamela Olivo as she interviews experts such as Iván Andrés Arana González and Ricardo Thierry. Throughout this conversation, we will learn how simulators can provide professionals with specific tools to lead business strategies and incorporate new knowledge into their daily practice. Join us on this enriching experience, and let's discover how to improve our logistics skills together. Let's learn about logistics from experts!

OER: Proposal for a Participatory Methodology for the Creation of Serious Games
Authors: Ernesto Armando Pacheco-Velázquez, Lucia Rabago Mayer, Andre Bester & Virginia Rodés Paragarino
Reference: Pacheco-Velázquez, E., Bester, A., Rabago Mayer, L., & Rodes-Paragarino, V. (2023). Proposal for a Participatory Methodology for the Creation of Serious Games. In *European Conference on Games Based Learning 17*(1), 475–481. https://repositorio.tec.mx/handle/11285/653799

▶ Let's explore this educational text resource presented at an international conference, which addresses a fascinating and very current topic. Technology has changed the way people relate to the world, and, in the educational field, it is seen as a tool that facilitates learning and develops skills. In this context, simulators and serious games emerge as effective strategies to facilitate learning. The benefits of serious games are obvious: they encourage critical thinking and creativity, improve problem-solving skills and increase information retention. However, these games must be well-designed to maintain their appeal and playful essence. The article I invite you to read discusses the importance of establishing clear specifications and requirements before moving on to the development, implementation or evaluation phases of these games. It discusses how the lack of a proper design methodology and ambiguity in requirements can affect the effectiveness of serious games. This resource is crucial to understanding how to create effective educational games that truly impact student learning. Let's discover how technology can transform education together!

CALL TO ACTION

We'd love to hear from you and learn together!
The challenges of our time can only be overcome through collaboration and by harnessing the value of diversity. Therefore, we invite you to participate in the project by reviewing the contact section at the following link of the V-Logistics platform: https://v-logistics.co/contact-us. Whether you have projects you want to explore, research to do, ideas to develop, or communities to inspire, we're here to support you. We want to build collaboratively with you, whether you are part of civil society, a school, a university, a company or a decision-making group. Each sector has a unique and valuable perspective to bring to the future of education.

Join us and let's build a better future together!
Our research group: https://tec.mx/es/r4c-irg
Explore our projects: https://www.research4challenges.world/

Join V-Logistics:
https://www.research4challenges.world/s4l-1 project

GLOSSARY

Logistics: Logistics is the process of moving and storing products from where they are made to where they are needed. This includes activities such as transporting, storing and managing inventories to make sure products reach customers efficiently.

Supply Chain: The supply chain is the set of organisations that a product goes through and the stages it follows from the time the raw material is obtained until it reaches the end customer. This includes the production, storage, distribution and delivery of the product and requires that everything works in a coordinated manner to meet consumer demand.

Sustainable Development Goals (SDGs): The SDGs are a set of global and concrete action-oriented goals whose purpose is to protect the planet, eradicate poverty and achieve peace and prosperity for all people. Each SDG includes several specific targets that detail how to achieve each goal, promoting a comprehensive approach to sustainable development around the world.

Complex Thinking: Complex thinking is the competence of observing reality by considering the totality of the factors that converge to shape it. Rather than focusing on each factor in isolation, it is understood that each part contributes to and is influenced by the totality of reality. This integrative approach allows us to understand how the different parts are interrelated and affect each other, providing a more complete and in-depth view of the world.

Contenido

Aprendamos Logística a Través de la Simulación

Plataforma S4L

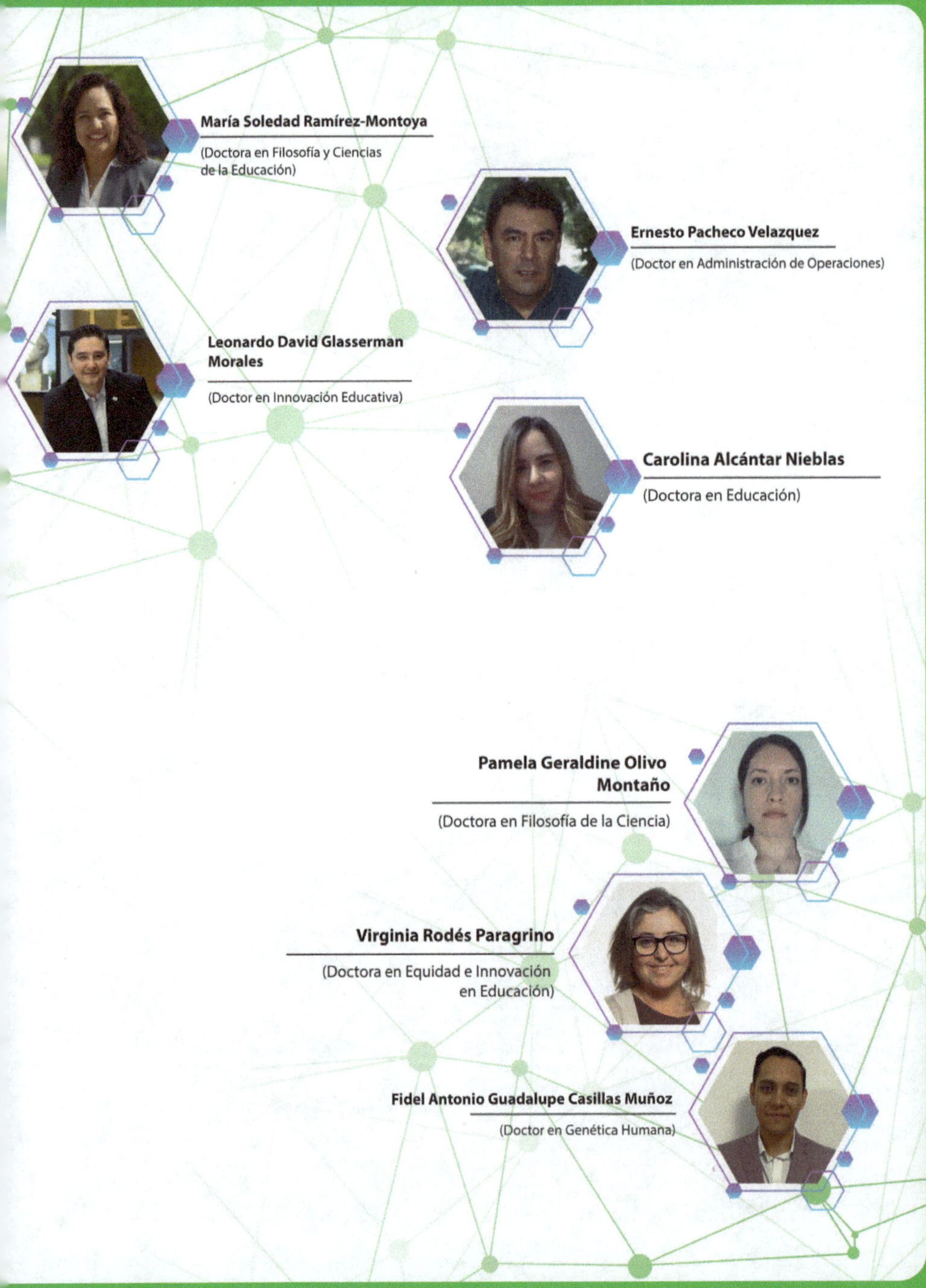

Figura 1.
Investigadores del R4C-IRG, movilizadores de la plataforma S4L

Sobre Nosotros

Somos integrantes del grupo de investigación R4C-IRG Escalando el Pensamiento Complejo para Todos (Figura 1), nos apasiona llevar la educación superior a nuevos niveles de excelencia. Nos dedicamos a desarrollar y promover competencias avanzadas de razonamiento para enfrentar la complejidad del mundo moderno. Utilizamos estrategias de ciencia abierta y las más avanzadas tecnologías 5.0, como la inteligencia artificial y la ciencia de datos, para crear sistemas formativos que preparen a las personas para los desafíos del futuro. Nuestra labor se enlaza con proyectos que integran la universidad, la industria, el gobierno y el sector civil, buscando siempre soluciones sostenibles que beneficien a toda la sociedad.

Nuestra visión es clara y ambiciosa: contribuir de manera significativa al futuro de la educación, creando soluciones innovadoras para los problemas y retos de la sociedad actual. Nos alineamos con los objetivos de la agenda 2030 de la UNESCO para el desarrollo sostenible, fomentando la colaboración interdisciplinaria y la construcción de redes académicas robustas. En R4C-IRG, trabajamos para formar una nueva generación de profesionales altamente competitivos y comprometidos con el bienestar social, siempre buscando habilitar soluciones innovadoras que respondan a los retos presentes y futuros.

Carta Editorial

Estamos emocionados de compartir contigo nuestra visión para diseñar una plataforma educativa innovadora que actúa como un sistema de gestión de contenidos de aprendizaje, desde el cual se facilita la creación, gestión y distribución de contenido educativo. Esta plataforma valida el desarrollo de competencias en razonamiento para la complejidad y aprendizaje autorregulado en sus usuarios, como estudiantes, personal académico, personas tomadoras de decisiones y representantes del sector empresarial. Nuestro objetivo es apoyar en la formación de profesionales capaces de enfrentar las necesidades de aprendizaje a lo largo de la vida, preparándolos para los desafíos actuales y futuros.

El proyecto S4L (Simulation for Learning) es significativo porque busca fomentar la competitividad en la industria de la logística, con instancias formativas que favorezcan a las personas la toma de decisiones de manera más eficiente. Este enfoque no solo mejora las habilidades individuales, sino que también contribuye al desarrollo del sector. Las personas usuarias de la plataforma pueden adquirir conocimientos de manera lúdica, observar las consecuencias de cada decisión, identificar las variables principales que influyen en un proceso real y desarrollar una motivación intrínseca para investigar, entender y experimentar con nuevas estrategias que optimicen la solución de problemas. Nuestros principales objetivos de impacto de este proyecto son gobiernos, asociaciones profesionales, ONG y el sector empresarial.

¡Te invitamos a participar en la plataforma que transforma la manera en que aprendemos y resolvemos problemas, preparándonos para un futuro más brillante y eficiente!

OBJETIVOS

Nuestro objetivo principal es desarrollar una plataforma de sistema de gestión de contenidos de aprendizaje que, utilizando herramientas de la industria 5.0 como computación en la nube, inteligencia artificial, simulaciones, juegos serios, biometría, análisis de datos y recursos abiertos, promueva el razonamiento complejo y las habilidades de aprendizaje autorregulado. Esta plataforma proporciona indicadores cuantitativos y cualitativos sobre el comportamiento de los usuarios, con el fin de formar profesionales capaces de adaptarse y aprender de manera continua, brindando la preparación adecuada para los desafíos de un mundo en constante cambio.

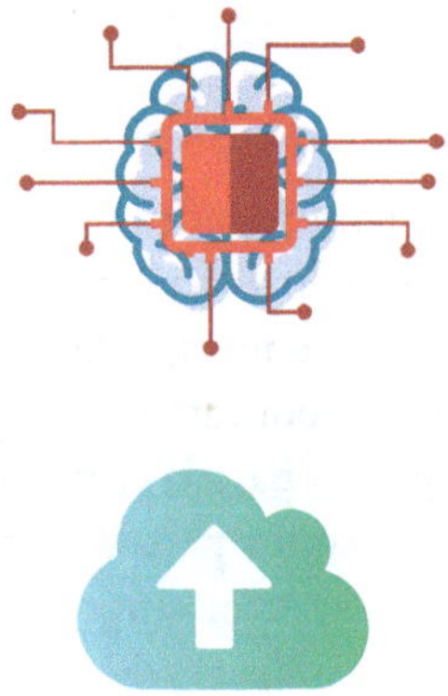

OBJETIVOS ESPECÍFICOS

1. Seleccionar, desde un equipo interdisciplinario, las características esenciales que garanticen que la plataforma fomente el desarrollo de competencias específicas, como el pensamiento complejo. Esto permite configurar adecuadamente su diseño y arquitectura.

2. Analizar el funcionamiento de la primera versión de la plataforma para determinar su eficacia en el desarrollo del razonamiento complejo y el aprendizaje autorregulado. Para la evaluación se utilizan los instrumentos seleccionados, y a partir de los resultados, se valorará la experiencia de las personas usuarias para realizar mejoras.

3. Validar la plataforma con personas socias estratégicas y se registra la propuesta de la plataforma. Finalmente, se realiza un proceso de transferencia a diversos sectores y partes interesadas.

Figura 2.
Objetivos generales y específicos de la plataforma S4L

Objetivos

Introducción

En la década de los 80 (del siglo pasado), descubrí una película protagonizada por Tom Hanks llamada *Quisiera ser grande* (o "Big"). En esta película, el personaje principal, Josh Baskin, es un niño atrapado en el cuerpo de un adulto que sueña con un juego interactivo donde los participantes puedan cambiar o crear personajes, darles diferentes características, y construir sus propias historias. La idea consiste en la creación de un *software* en el que las personas puedan encontrar una historia diferente con solo cambiar algunos detalles en la caracterización de los personajes.

Durante muchos años, me he dedicado a la enseñanza de la toma de decisiones en el terreno logístico, y siempre he considerado que la logística parece un juego de estrategia donde cada elección impacta en el resultado final. Al igual que en un juego, los gestores logísticos deben considerar múltiples variables, como la selección de proveedores, la ubicación de fábricas y la gestión de centros de distribución y tiendas. Cada decisión debe ser cuidadosamente analizada y ajustada en respuesta a cambios en el entorno (Kong, 2021), tal como un jugador de estrategia adapta sus movimientos para superar desafíos y alcanzar sus objetivos. Cuando las características de algunas de las variables cambian, es muy posible que los resultados obtenidos al seguir una determinada estrategia también se modifiquen.

El proyecto de investigación Simulation for Learning (S4L) fue el punto de partida para el desarrollo de la plataforma de simulación logística llamada V-Logistics. A través de S4L, se exploraron métodos de aprendizaje experiencial en entornos virtuales para mejorar la comprensión y la toma de decisiones en logística. Los hallazgos y las metodologías diseñadas en S4L sirvieron como base para crear V-Logistics, una herramienta que permite a los usuarios modelar y simular entornos logísticos en 3D. La relación entre ambos es fundamental, ya que V-Logistics aplica los principios de S4L al ofrecer un entorno de simulación interactivo, optimizado para el aprendizaje y la práctica en logística, promoviendo así la transferencia de conocimiento a través de experiencias simuladas realistas.

El proyecto nació de la necesidad de abordar las limitaciones de los métodos tradicionales de enseñanza en logística, que a menudo son demasiado teóricos y no reflejan la complejidad y dinamismo del mundo real. Nuestra innovación busca llenar este vacío proporcionando una herramienta que simula un entorno logístico real, permitiendo a cada estudiante aprender haciendo y adaptarse a diferentes escenarios y desafíos.

V-Logistics es una plataforma educativa que permite a quienes participan en ella, diseñar y gestionar su propia cadena logística. En esta plataforma, las personas usuarias pueden elegir el giro del negocio, definir el número de proveedores, fábricas, centros de distribución, tiendas, y personalizar las características de cada uno de estos elementos (Pacheco-Velázquez et al., 2023). La idea es que cada participante pueda experimentar y aprender sobre logística de una manera práctica y dinámica, similar a cómo Josh, el de la película, imaginó su juego.

En tanto, el proyecto Simulación para el Aprendizaje (S4L) inició con la visión de aportar a la supervivencia de las pequeñas empresas y la calidad de vida de los habitantes, colaborando con diferentes actores de la sociedad para la creación de diversos escenarios de acuerdo con la realidad de cada región (Figura 3). El principal objetivo de nuestro proyecto, representado a través de la plataforma V-Logistics, es mejorar la comprensión y habilidades de cada persona en logística y optimización ofreciendo una experiencia de aprendizaje interactiva y personalizada. Esperamos que quienes participen no solo adquieran conocimientos teóricos, sino que también desarrollen habilidades prácticas al enfrentarse a situaciones reales y tomar decisiones que afecten el desempeño de su cadena logística.

La relevancia de esta propuesta se sustenta en investigaciones que subrayan la importancia del aprendizaje experiencial y la gamificación en la educación. Estudios han demostrado que se retiene más información y se desarrollan mejores habilidades cuando se participa activamente en el proceso de aprendizaje. Al ofrecer un entorno de aprendizaje donde se puede experimentar y aprender de las propias decisiones, nuestro *software* aborda de manera efectiva los problemas de desconexión entre teoría y práctica que han persistido en la enseñanza de la logística. Beneficiará a diversos grupos de estudiantes, incluyendo aquellos con necesidades especiales o en contextos desfavorecidos, al proporcionar una

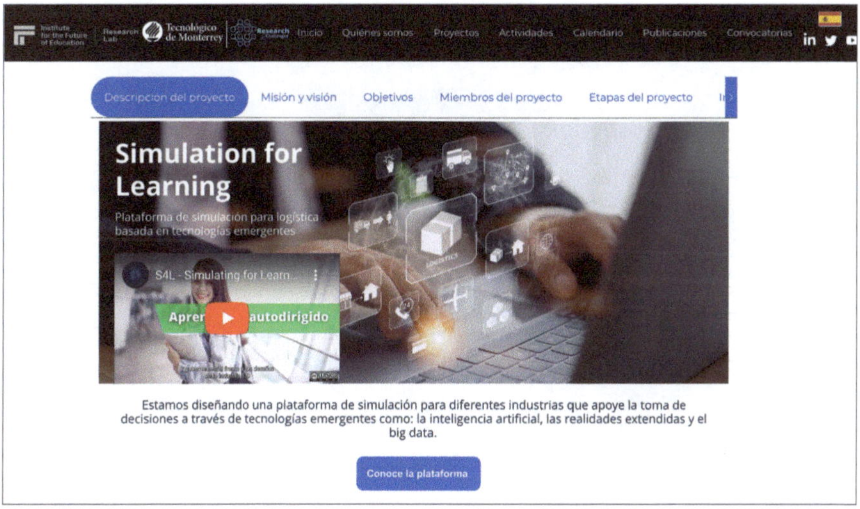

Figura 3. Página web del proyecto S4L (https://www.research4challenges.world/s4l-1)

herramienta accesible y adaptable a diferentes estilos de aprendizaje y niveles de habilidad. Cada estudiante podrá ver en tiempo real cómo sus decisiones impactan la cadena logística, fomentando un aprendizaje profundo y significativo.

Nuestro proyecto tiene el potencial de transformar la educación en logística, proporcionando una herramienta innovadora que combina teoría y práctica de manera interactiva. La personalización y la flexibilidad que ofrece la plataforma no solo mejora la experiencia de aprendizaje, sino que también prepara a las personas a enfrentar los desafíos del mundo real. La importancia de seguir innovando en la educación es crucial para preparar a las nuevas generaciones para un futuro cada vez más complejo y dinámico.

Referencias

Kong, Y. (2021). The role of experiential learning on students' motivation and classroom engagement. *Frontiers in Psychology*, https://doi.org/10.3389/fpsyg.2021.771272

Pacheco-Velázquez, E., Salinas-Navarro, D. E., y Ramírez-Montoya, M. S. (2023). Serious Games and Experiential Learning: Options for Engineering Education. *International Journal of Serious Games, 10*(3), 3–21 https://doi.org/10.17083/ijsg.v10i3.593

¿Cómo se Vincula el Pensamiento Complejo Con Procesos De Logística?

El pensamiento complejo es una habilidad que nos permite ver los problemas y situaciones desde una perspectiva amplia e interconectada. En lugar de dividir todo en partes aisladas, nos ayuda a entender cómo todas las piezas de un sistema se relacionan e influyen entre sí. Es como ver un bosque completo en lugar de solo mirar árbol por árbol. Este enfoque combina diferentes formas de pensar: ver patrones (sistémico), basarse en hechos y pruebas (científico), analizar de forma crítica (crítico) y encontrar soluciones creativas (innovador). Al adoptar el pensamiento complejo, podemos tomar decisiones más informadas y efectivas en cualquier aspecto de nuestra vida.

Ahora, imagina aplicar esta poderosa combinación en el campo de la logística. La logística implica planificar, implementar y controlar de manera eficiente el flujo y almacenamiento de bienes, servicios e información desde el origen hasta el consumo, asegurando la satisfacción del cliente. Usar el pensamiento complejo en logística significa ver todo el proceso como un sistema interconectado, usando datos y evidencia para tomar decisiones, evaluando constantemente las estrategias y buscando siempre maneras innovadoras de mejorar.

La competencia de pensamiento complejo se revela como fundamental en el desarrollo de habilidades para la logística, un campo que requiere la gestión eficaz de múltiples variables interconectadas en tiempo real. En logística, el pensamiento complejo permite a las personas profesionales entender y optimizar la cadena de suministro desde una perspectiva holística, anticipando cómo los cambios en un área pueden impactar en otras. Por ejemplo, puede ayudar a prever el efecto de un retraso en el transporte sobre los niveles de inventario o la satisfacción de cada cliente, facilitando decisiones rápidas y fundamentadas. Este enfoque integrador no solo mejora la eficiencia operativa, sino que también potencia la capacidad de innovación en la creación de soluciones logísticas que se adapten a los desafíos emergentes, como las fluctuaciones del mercado o las interrupciones globales.

PARA SABER MÁS ...
sobre pensamiento complejo y procesos de logística

Pensar la complejidad. Crisis y metamorfosis

Autor: Edgar Morin.

Referencia: Morin, E. (2010). *Pensar la complejidad. Crisis y metamorfosis.* Universidad de Valencia.

▶ Hoy quiero invitarte a descubrir un estudio apasionante que conecta el pensamiento complejo con los procesos de logística, dos áreas que, combinadas, pueden transformar nuestra comprensión y gestión del mundo. El pensamiento complejo nos ayuda a ver las conexiones e interacciones entre diversas partes de un sistema, permitiéndonos abordar problemas con una visión integral y multidisciplinaria. Ahora, imagina aplicar esta forma de pensar en la logística, donde planificamos y controlamos el flujo de bienes, servicios e información. Para profundizar en esta fascinante perspectiva, te invitamos a leer *Pensar la complejidad. Crisis y metamorfosis* de Edgar Morin. Este libro es una ventana al pensamiento transdisciplinario de Morin, que combina conocimientos de diversas disciplinas como la física, la biología y la ética. Su enfoque innovador nos enseña a ver más allá de los compartimentos del conocimiento y a comprender la complejidad de los fenómenos sociales y naturales.

Exploring educational simulation platform features for addressing complexity in Industry 4.0: a qualitative analysis of insights from logistics experts

Autores: Ernesto Pacheco-Velázquez, Virginia Rodés Paragarino y Alberto Marquez-Uribe.

Referencia: Pacheco-Velázquez, E., Rodés, V., y Marquez-Uribe, A. (2023). Exploring Educational Simulation Platform Features for Addressing Complexity in Industry 4.0: A Qualitative Analysis of Insights from Logistics Experts. *Frontiers in Education.* https://doi.org/10.3389/feduc.2024.1331911 https://repositorio.tec.mx/handle/11285/652447

▶ Para aprender más te recomendamos este fabuloso estudio que examina cómo la Industria 4.0, con tecnologías como la inteligencia artificial y el análisis de grandes datos, está transformando las operaciones industriales y la logística, resaltando los desafíos y la necesidad de nuevas herramientas para gestionar la complejidad. A través del diseño y uso de simuladores logísticos adaptados a la Industria 4.0, se busca equipar a los profesionales con las competencias necesarias para mejorar la toma de decisiones y la planificación operativa en este entorno tecnológicamente avanzado.

Modelo abierto de pensamiento complejo para el futuro de la educación

Autores: María Soledad Ramírez- Montoya, Fabián Eduardo Basabe, Martina Carlos Arroyo, Irma Azeneth Patiño Zúñiga, I. A. y May Portuguez Castro.

Referencia: Ramírez-Montoya, M. S., Basabe, F. E., Carlos Arroyo, M., Patiño Zúñiga, I. A. y Portuguez Castro, M. (2024). *Modelo abierto de pensamiento complejo para el futuro de la educación*. Octaedro. https://hdl.handle.net/11285/652033

▶ Para descubrir más sobre pensamiento complejo, te invitamos a explorar un enfoque educativo innovador que se presenta en este texto. Este enfoque está diseñado para responder a las demandas del mundo moderno, integrando diversas dimensiones del pensamiento —crítico, científico, sistémico e innovador—. El objetivo es formar ciudadanos empáticos y comprometidos con el desarrollo sostenible. Este modelo no solo se aplica en ambientes académicos, sino también en sectores gubernamentales y empresariales, destacando la importancia de la colaboración, la empatía y el compromiso con soluciones sostenibles a problemas globales. Al sumergirte en este enfoque, podrás desarrollar habilidades que te permitirán contribuir de manera significativa a la sociedad y al bienestar del planeta.

Innovación Educativa en Acción

La plataforma V-Logistics es una herramienta educativa que transforma la manera de enseñar y aprender sobre logística, operaciones y cadenas de suministro. Utiliza casos de estudio y escenarios específicos para mejorar habilidades importantes como el pensamiento complejo y el aprendizaje autónomo. Esta plataforma no solo presenta información, sino que también ayuda a las personas usuarias a desarrollar y afinar sus competencias críticas a través de la práctica y la interacción con contenido relevante.

V-Logistics se caracteriza por:

- Contenido educativo multimodal: incluye una amplia gama de materiales didácticos, como videos, tutoriales, infografías y recursos interactivos. Se promueve el acceso abierto donde algunos materiales se generan como recursos educativos abiertos (REA). Los recursos se encuentran disponibles en idioma español o inglés.
- Evaluaciones y seguimiento del progreso: permite a las personas usuarias evaluar su comprensión de los contenidos y progreso con respecto al desarrollo de competencias de pensamiento complejo y del aprendizaje autorregulado, a través de cuestionarios y pruebas en línea, además de la visualización de resultados por medio de tableros informativos.
- Escalable: permite adecuar contenidos o actividades específicas de formación con base en las necesidades de los grupos de interés.

A través de la plataforma se ofrece un acompañamiento integral con el apoyo de un mapa de navegación, que muestra diferentes ambientes de aprendizaje que fomentan la toma de decisiones pertinentes, fundamentadas y consecuentes a los objetivos de aprendizaje esperados (crear redes logísticas, jugar de manera libre, realizar una autoevaluación a través de rutas de aprendizaje).

La plataforma opera como un agregador de contenidos que se apoya de los componentes:

· V-Logistics Editor

Entorno interactivo y flexible para que las personas usuarias diseñen sus propias redes y situaciones logísticas. Esta herramienta fomenta la creatividad y la aplicación práctica de conocimientos teóricos en logística, permitiendo a los usuarios personalizar contextos y escenarios según sus necesidades de aprendizaje.

Tiene las siguientes características:

Interfaz intuitiva: facilita la creación de redes logísticas con una interfaz de usuario amigable y fácil de usar.	**Personalización de E escenarios:** permite a cada estudiante diseñar escenarios logísticos personalizados, ajustando variables y parámetros para crear desafíos únicos.	**Herramientas versátiles:** incluye una variedad de herramientas y recursos para simular diferentes aspectos de la logística, como transporte, almacenamiento, y gestión de inventarios.	**Visualización de datos:** ofrece capacidades avanzadas de visualización para ayudar a cada estudiante a comprender mejor la estructura y el funcionamiento de las redes logísticas.

· V-Logistics Simulador (entorno de simulación)

Es un entorno diseñado para simular y ejecutar las redes logísticas creadas en V-Logistics Editor. Su objetivo es facilitar la comprensión de las interfaces en una red logística con una experiencia interactiva donde las personas usuarias puedan probar sus diseños, estrategias, y tomar decisiones en tiempo real, enfrentando los desafíos de la gestión logística.

V-Logistics Simulador tiene las siguientes características:

Simulación realista: ejecuta las redes logísticas con un alto nivel de realismo, mostrando cómo las decisiones afectan el sistema en tiempo real.	**Interactividad y toma de decisiones:** permite a las personas usuarias interactuar con el escenario, tomando decisiones y ajustando estrategias sobre la marcha.	**Retroalimentación instantánea:** muestra resultados inmediatos del impacto de las decisiones tomadas, permitiendo un aprendizaje iterativo y reflexivo.	**Adaptabilidad a diferentes escenarios:** capaz de manejar una amplia gama de situaciones logísticas diseñadas.

V-Logistics hace uso de otras tecnologías emergentes para mejorar la experiencia de aprendizaje de las personas usuarias, pudiendo ser estudiantes de educación superior, profesionales en diferentes sectores de la industria, gobierno, sociedad civil o academia, por lo que puede ser utilizada en espacios de educación formal y de aprendizaje permanente. En la educación formal, complementa el currículo tradicional proporcionando acceso a recursos adicionales y oportunidades de aprendizaje interactivo. Para las empresas y organizaciones es una plataforma ideal para la formación continua y el desarrollo profesional.

Al iniciar sesión en V-Logistics

Una vez iniciada la sesión en la plataforma, la persona usuaria observa el mapa de navegación, que organiza los diferentes apartados de la siguiente manera:

a) Inicia aquí: este entorno describe la plataforma como un recurso LCMS y gestiona diferentes secciones.
b) Crea tu red logística: aquí, se puede construir una propia red logística utilizando V-Logistics Editor. Puede crear un nuevo juego, jugar un juego disponible previamente creado o continuar un juego que se inició, pero no se completó.
c) Juegos gratis: esta sección lista juegos que pueden revisarse y jugarse de manera libre. Las condiciones de estos juegos están preestablecidas por cada diseñador.
d) Rutas de aprendizaje: esta es la sección central de V-Logistics, donde se presentan las intenciones pedagógicas de un trayecto formativo. Incluye instrumentos de preevaluación, secuencias didácticas y casos que guían a la persona usuaria en lo que debe realizar. También ofrece un entorno generador de juegos, recursos educativos abiertos en formato de video, infografías, casos, manuales, glosario, y herramientas de evaluación del desarrollo de competencias de pensamiento complejo, aprendizaje autorregulado, experiencia de juego y experiencia de usuario. Al completar todas las actividades de una ruta de aprendizaje, cada persona usuaria puede solicitar una constancia digital, validada por el equipo de administración de V-Logistics.
e) Resultados: en esta sección, las personas usuarias que completaron una ruta de aprendizaje pueden revisar sus resultados respecto al desarrollo de competencias de pensamiento complejo, aprendizaje autorregulado, experiencia de juego y experiencia de usuario. La información se presenta en tableros informativos.
f) Contáctanos: esta sección facilita diferentes intenciones y canales de comunicación entre las personas usuarias y el equipo de V-Logistics.
g) Recursos educativos: aquí se categorizan los diferentes recursos incluidos en las actividades de la plataforma V-Logistics (videos, videos 360°, casos, infografías, secuencias didácticas, entre otros).
h) Testimonios: esta sección presenta la vinculación con representantes de diferentes sectores y las voces de algunos usuarios.

Análisis de V-Logistics

Algunos elementos que podrían incorporarse a V-Logistics para mejorar su funcionamiento y enriquecer la experiencia de aprendizaje:

1. Simulación de incidentes y contingencias
   - Descripción: incorporar eventos aleatorios o programados, como desastres naturales, huelgas, fallas en la cadena de suministro, o fluctuaciones en el precio de los insumos.
   - Beneficio: estos eventos ayudarían a los estudiantes a desarrollar habilidades de gestión de riesgos y a tomar decisiones en situaciones de crisis, preparándolos para enfrentar incertidumbre en entornos reales.
2. Análisis de sostenibilidad y huella de carbono
   - Descripción: agregar módulos para calcular el impacto ambiental de las decisiones logísticas, como el consumo de energía, emisiones de CO_2 y residuos.
   - Beneficio: facilitaría la enseñanza de logística sostenible y el compromiso con prácticas responsables, alineándose con los Objetivos de Desarrollo Sostenible (ODS) y sensibilizando a los estudiantes sobre la importancia de minimizar el impacto ambiental.
3. Inteligencia artificial para predicción de demanda y optimización
   - Descripción: incorporar algoritmos de IA que permitan predecir la demanda y optimizar las decisiones de inventario, producción y distribución en función de patrones históricos y de demanda.
   - Beneficio: los estudiantes podrían ver cómo la IA apoya la toma de decisiones y aprender a aplicar tecnología avanzada en la cadena de suministro, desarrollando habilidades para interpretar y ajustar las recomendaciones de estos algoritmos.
4. Integración de finanzas y presupuestos
   - Descripción: agregar un componente financiero que permita a los usuarios ver el impacto de sus decisiones logísticas en costos operativos, márgenes de ganancia, y retorno de inversión.
   - Beneficio: esta función permitiría a los estudiantes entender la relación entre las decisiones logísticas y el rendimiento financiero de la empresa, promoviendo una perspectiva integral de la gestión empresarial.
5. Personalización de roles y responsabilidades en equipos
   - Descripción: implementar la posibilidad de que los estudiantes asuman roles específicos (por ejemplo, gerente de inventarios, jefe de transporte, analista de compras) y coordinen sus acciones para alcanzar los objetivos del equipo.
   - Beneficio: esto facilitaría el desarrollo de habilidades de trabajo en equipo y comunicación, así como la comprensión de cómo se relacionan y afectan los diferentes roles en una cadena de suministro.

6. Módulo de toma de decisiones basada en indicadores clave de desempeño (KPI)
    - Descripción: incluir una sección que permita a los usuarios desarrollar, monitorear e interpretar indicadores clave de desempeño (KPI) en tiempo real, como tiempo de ciclo, nivel de servicio, o índice de cumplimiento de pedidos.
    - Beneficio: los estudiantes podrían practicar la gestión basada en datos, evaluando continuamente el desempeño de la cadena de suministro y tomando decisiones informadas.
7. Simulación de comercio internacional y legislación aduanera
    - Descripción: incorporar escenarios que incluyan aspectos de comercio internacional, como aranceles, tiempos de despacho aduanero y regulaciones de importación/exportación.
    - Beneficio: permitirá a los estudiantes comprender las complejidades del comercio global y cómo las barreras arancelarias y las políticas regulatorias pueden afectar el flujo de productos.
8. Gamificación y retroalimentación inmediata
    - Descripción: añadir elementos de gamificación, como logros, niveles y recompensas, junto con retroalimentación inmediata sobre las decisiones tomadas.
    - Beneficio: incrementaría la motivación y el compromiso de los estudiantes, proporcionándoles incentivos para mejorar continuamente y aprender de los errores de forma interactiva.
9. Visualización avanzada de flujos y mapas logísticos
    - Descripción: desarrollar visualizaciones dinámicas de los flujos logísticos en un mapa interactivo, con opciones de seguimiento en tiempo real de envíos, inventarios y rutas de transporte.
    - Beneficio: esta función facilitará el análisis de la red logística y permitiría a los estudiantes comprender mejor el impacto espacial de sus decisiones, ayudando en la optimización de rutas y distribución de recursos.
10. Escenarios de negociación con proveedores y clientes
    - Descripción: incluir opciones de negociación que permitan a los estudiantes interactuar con proveedores y clientes, ajustando términos de entrega, precios y niveles de servicio.
    - Beneficio: ayudaría a desarrollar habilidades de negociación y comunicación efectiva, esenciales en la gestión de relaciones en la cadena de suministro.
11. Incorporación de realidad aumentada (RA)
    - Descripción: utilizar RA para visualizar y manipular elementos de la cadena de suministro, como inventarios y flujo de materiales en un entorno tridimensional.

- Beneficio: ofrecería una experiencia inmersiva que ayudaría a los estudiantes a visualizar procesos logísticos complejos, mejorando la comprensión espacial y el análisis de la disposición de la cadena de suministro.

Comparación de V-Logistics con otras plataformas similares

1. Simulación realista de entornos logísticos
   - V-Logistics. Está diseñado específicamente para brindar una experiencia realista, integrando áreas clave de la empresa (proveedores, fábricas, centros de distribución, tiendas, clientes mayoristas), lo que permite a los estudiantes experimentar un flujo logístico completo y entender la interdependencia entre las áreas.
   - The Beer Game: Aunque es un juego popular para enseñar conceptos básicos de cadena de suministro y el efecto látigo, se enfoca más en el flujo de información y la gestión de inventarios en una cadena sencilla de cuatro actores. No permite la personalización de escenarios ni la integración de múltiples áreas funcionales como V-Logistics.
   - Simulador de Cadena de Suministro de MIT (SCM Globe). Permite a los estudiantes diseñar y operar redes de cadena de suministro en escenarios globales, pero generalmente se enfoca en la planificación estratégica y menos en la interacción entre áreas operativas específicas.
2. Personalización y adaptabilidad de escenarios
   - V-Logistics. Permite la creación de escenarios personalizados, donde los usuarios pueden elegir el tipo de negocio, definir el número de proveedores, fábricas y centros de distribución, lo que facilita una experiencia de aprendizaje adaptada a distintos contextos y objetivos de estudio.
   - Logistics Simulator (LLamasoft). Ofrece una simulación avanzada de redes de cadena de suministro, pero está más orientado hacia el análisis de datos y la optimización de redes grandes, con menos enfoque en la enseñanza paso a paso o la interacción directa de los estudiantes en la configuración de escenarios.
   - SAP ERPsim. Simula la gestión empresarial en un entorno ERP, donde los estudiantes toman decisiones de ventas, producción e inventarios. Sin embargo, su nivel de personalización de escenarios es más limitado y requiere conocimientos previos de ERP para aprovechar plenamente la experiencia.
3. Énfasis en el aprendizaje experiencial y adaptativo
   - V-Logistics. Fomenta el aprendizaje "haciendo", permitiendo a los estudiantes adaptarse a cambios en el mercado, ajustes en la demanda y problemas en la cadena de suministro, promoviendo habilidades de toma de decisiones en situaciones complejas.

- Inchainge's The Fresh Connection. Permite a los estudiantes tomar decisiones en un entorno de cadena de suministro, especialmente en la industria de alimentos, donde experimentan las consecuencias de sus decisiones en una cadena integrada. Sin embargo, su adaptabilidad a otros sectores y su enfoque se centra principalmente en la gestión de inventarios y compras.
- Business on the Move. Un juego de mesa educativo que enseña conceptos logísticos básicos, orientado a niveles educativos iniciales. No posee la adaptabilidad ni profundidad de escenarios de V-Logistics, aunque es efectivo para introducir a los estudiantes a conceptos básicos de logística y transporte.

4. Integración de variables operativas y estratégicas
   - V-Logistics. Proporciona una perspectiva integral al integrar decisiones operativas, como selección de proveedores y gestión de almacenes, con aspectos estratégicos como la expansión de la red de distribución o la diversificación de productos, lo que ofrece una visión completa del negocio.
   - Littlefield Technologies. Es un simulador que permite a los estudiantes gestionar una planta de producción, optimizando recursos en un entorno de manufactura. Aunque proporciona una visión detallada de la producción, no cubre la cadena de suministro completa ni integra áreas funcionales diversas como lo hace V-Logistics.
5. Desarrollo de indicadores personalizados
   - V-Logistics. Alienta a los estudiantes a desarrollar e interpretar indicadores logísticos específicos, facilitando la práctica de análisis de datos y la creación de métricas personalizadas para evaluar el desempeño de sus cadenas de suministro.
   - Simuladores como SCM Globe y LLamasoft. Ofrecen herramientas de análisis de datos e indicadores predeterminados, pero su personalización para crear nuevos indicadores es limitada y generalmente requiere experiencia técnica avanzada.

Característica	V-Logistics	The Beer Game	SCM Globe	SAP ERPsim	The Fresh Connection	Business on the Move	Littlefield Technologies
Realismo del entorno logístico	Alto	Medio	Medio-Alto	Alto	Alto	Bajo	Medio
Personalización de escenarios	Alta	Baja	Media	Media	Baja	Baja	Media
Enfoque en aprendizaje experiencial	Alto	Medio	Medio	Medio	Alto	Bajo	Medio
Integración de áreas funcionales	Completa	Limitada	Parcial	Parcial	Parcial	Limitada	Enfoque en producción
Indicadores personalizados	Alta	No	Limitada	Limitada	Limitada	No	Limitada

¿QUÉ DICEN LOS ESTUDIOS ...

sobre la propuesta que se realiza desde el proyecto de innovación?

La implementación de simulaciones logísticas y el aprendizaje basado en juegos (GBL) en la educación ha demostrado tener un impacto significativo en el desarrollo de habilidades críticas y competencias esenciales en los estudiantes (Kokkalia, 2017; Zhonggen, 2019). Utilizando plataformas de simulación, los estudiantes pueden enfrentarse a escenarios complejos y dinámicos que replican situaciones del mundo real, promoviendo así el pensamiento crítico y la toma de decisiones informadas. Estas herramientas no solo mejoran la comprensión de los procesos logísticos y la gestión de la cadena de suministro, sino que también fomentan la autogestión y la autonomía en el aprendizaje. Los estudios han revelado que los estudiantes que participan en simulaciones logísticas desarrollan una mayor apertura a nuevas oportunidades de aprendizaje, iniciativa e independencia en su proceso educativo y una percepción más robusta de sí mismos como aprendices efectivos (Pacheco-Velázquez, 2022; Olexová y Gajdoš, 2016). Este enfoque, basado en la gamificación y el aprendizaje activo, resulta en una experiencia educativa más interactiva y envolvente, que prepara mejor a los estudiantes para los desafíos del mercado laboral contemporáneo.

Además, las simulaciones logísticas han mostrado ser particularmente efectivas en el fortalecimiento de las habilidades de aprendizaje autodirigido (SDL) (Pacheco-Velázquez, 2020). Mediante el uso de simulaciones, los estudiantes no solo adquieren conocimientos técnicos, sino que también desarrollan competencias transversales como la capacidad de analizar y resolver problemas complejos, la gestión del tiempo, y la habilidad para trabajar de manera colaborativa. Estos entornos de aprendizaje simulado proporcionan un espacio seguro para experimentar y aprender de los errores, lo que es crucial para el desarrollo de la resiliencia y la adaptabilidad. Los estudios indican que los participantes en simulaciones logísticas reportan un aumento significativo en su amor por el aprendizaje y su motivación intrínseca para explorar y entender nuevos conceptos (Pacheco-Velázquez et al., 2023). Además, las investigaciones subrayan que las simulaciones y los juegos serios son herramientas efectivas para enseñar habilidades complejas y técnicas avanzadas, cruciales para la Industria 4.0. En resumen, las simulaciones logísticas no solo mejoran el rendimiento académico y la comprensión de contenidos específicos, sino que también equipan a los estudiantes con las herramientas necesarias para un aprendizaje continuo y autónomo, preparándolos para enfrentar la complejidad y las demandas de la industria moderna.

Referencias

Kokkalia, G., Drigas, A., Economou, A., Roussos, P. y Choli, S. (2017). The use of serious games in preschool education. *International Journal of Emerging Technologies in Learning, 12*(11).

Zhonggen, Y. (2019). A meta-analysis of use of serious games in education over a decade. *International Journal of Computer Games Technology, 2019*(1), 4797032. https://doi.org/10.1155/2019/4797032.

Pacheco-Velázquez, E. (2022). Effects of the use of simulators and an online platform in logistics education. *International Journal on Interactive Design and Manufacturing (IJIDeM) 16*(2), 439–457.

Olexová, C. y Gajdoš, J. (2016). Logistics simulation game proposal–A tool for employees' induction. *Quality Innovation Prosperity, 20*(2), 53–68.

Pacheco-Velázquez, E. (2020, March). Using gamification to develop self-directed learning. En *Proceedings of the 2020 International Conference on Education Development and Studies* (pp. 1–5).

Pacheco-Velázquez, E., Salinas-Navarro, D. E. y Ramírez-Montoya, M. S. (2023). Serious Games and Experiential Learning: Options for Engineering Education. *International Journal of Serious Games, 10*(3), 3–21.

TE INVITAMOS A REFLEXIONAR ...

Te invitamos a reflexionar sobre los impactos y beneficios de la simulación logística en el aprendizaje basado en juegos. Considera las siguientes preguntas para profundizar en la propuesta de innovación educativa que se expone:

1. ¿De qué manera crees que el uso de simulaciones logísticas puede transformar la enseñanza tradicional en tu área de estudio o trabajo?

____

____

____

2. ¿Cómo pueden las simulaciones y el aprendizaje basado en juegos fomentar el desarrollo de habilidades de autogestión, pensamiento complejo y aprendizaje autodirigido en cada estudiante? *Considera las implicaciones de permitir a cada estudiante gestionar su propio proceso de aprendizaje y cómo esto puede influir en su capacidad para adaptarse a contextos laborales cambiantes y complejos.*

____

____

____

3. ¿Qué desafíos podrían surgir al implementar simulaciones logísticas en un entorno educativo y cómo podrían superarse? *Reconoce y analiza las posibles barreras tecnológicas, pedagógicas o institucionales que podrían presentarse y sugiere estrategias para abordar estos obstáculos y maximizar el impacto positivo.*

____

____

____

Impactos y beneficios de la simulación logística y el aprendizaje basado en juegos en la educación

¿Es posible la transformación de la enseñanza tradicional con simulaciones logísticas?

El uso de simulaciones logísticas puede revolucionar la enseñanza tradicional en varias áreas de estudio, especialmente en aquellas relacionadas con la logística, el comercio y la gestión de cadenas de suministro. Estas herramientas permiten a cada estudiante interactuar con escenarios realistas y dinámicos, promoviendo una comprensión más profunda de los conceptos teóricos. A través de la simulación, cada estudiante puede experimentar las consecuencias de sus decisiones en un entorno controlado, lo que facilita el aprendizaje práctico y la retención de conocimientos.

Comparado con los métodos educativos convencionales, donde la enseñanza es principalmente teórica y expositiva, la simulación logística ofrece una experiencia inmersiva y participativa. La integración de estas herramientas puede cambiar la dinámica de aprendizaje a través de una de las siguientes formas:

- Los estudiantes dejan de ser **receptores pasivos** de información para convertirse en participantes activos que toman decisiones y resuelven problemas.
- La aplicación práctica de **conceptos teóricos en situaciones simuladas** ayuda a consolidar el aprendizaje.
- Las simulaciones requieren que cada estudiante **analice datos, evalúe alternativas y tome decisiones** informadas.
- Muchas simulaciones logísticas se desarrollan en equipos, promoviendo el **trabajo en conjunto y el intercambio de ideas.**

¿Cómo se pueden desarrollar habilidades a través de simulaciones y aprendizaje basado en juegos?

Las simulaciones y el aprendizaje basado en juegos pueden fomentar significativamente el desarrollo de habilidades clave como la autogestión, el pensamiento complejo y el aprendizaje autodirigido. Al permitir a cada estudiante a gestionar su propio proceso de aprendizaje, estas herramientas:

- **Promueven la autogestión**: cada estudiante aprende a planificar, organizar y evaluar sus acciones dentro de la simulación, desarrollando habilidades de gestión del tiempo y de los recursos.
- **Fomentan el pensamiento complejo**: las simulaciones presentan problemas multifacéticos que requieren el análisis de múltiples variables y la consideración de diversas perspectivas, lo que estimula el pensamiento sistémico y la resolución de problemas complejos.
- **Impulsan el aprendizaje autodirigido**: cada estudiante debe buscar activamente información, probar diferentes enfoques y aprender de sus errores, lo que le enseña a ser autodidacta y a adaptarse a nuevos desafíos.

Estas habilidades son cruciales para el contexto social moderno, donde la adaptabilidad y la capacidad de gestionar entornos cambiantes y complejos son altamente valoradas.

¿Cuáles son los desafíos y estrategias para la implementación de simulaciones logísticas en la educación?

Implementar simulaciones logísticas en un entorno educativo presenta varios desafíos, entre los que se incluyen:

- La falta de acceso a tecnología adecuada, como computadoras y *software* especializado.
- Algunos docentes pueden mostrarse reacios a adoptar nuevas metodologías debido a la falta de familiaridad o a la percepción de que son complejas de implementar.
- Es necesario utilizar recursos para llevar a cabo una formación continua y crear comunidades.
- Las restricciones presupuestarias y la rigidez curricular pueden dificultar la integración de nuevas herramientas educativas; para abordar esto, es fundamental que las instituciones busquen financiamiento externo, como subvenciones, y trabajen en la flexibilización de los currículos.

Maximizar el impacto positivo de la simulación logística en la educación requiere un enfoque integral que combine inversión en tecnología, formación docente, flexibilidad institucional y métodos de evaluación innovadores. Al enfrentar estos desafíos, las simulaciones pueden transformar profundamente el aprendizaje, preparando a los estudiantes para enfrentar con éxito los retos del mundo laboral moderno.

ODS en la Educación

Fortaleciendo los ODS: la contribución de V-Logistics

Los objetivos de V-Logistics están alineados con el ODS 4, que se centra en garantizar una educación de calidad, inclusiva y equitativa. En V-Logistics, trabajamos para mejorar la calidad y eficacia en el desarrollo de estas capacidades.

Además, V-Logistics tiene como meta mejorar las habilidades de gestión y toma de decisiones, lo que contribuye al crecimiento económico sostenible y la creación de empleos decentes. Esto se relaciona directamente con el ODS 8, que establece metas para un trabajo decente y crecimiento económico sostenido, inclusivo y sostenible, con empleo pleno y productivo para todas las personas.

Figura 4. ODS movilizados a través de la Plataforma S4L

V-Logistics también actúa como una herramienta para definir las operaciones logísticas de las empresas, vinculándose con el ODS 9, que se enfoca en la industria, innovación e infraestructura (Figura 4). Este objetivo busca construir infraestructuras resilientes, promover la industrialización inclusiva y sostenible, y fomentar la innovación.

PARA SABER MÁS ...

El vínculo entre los ODS y la propuesta

Informe de los Objetivos de Desarrollo Sostenible 2020

Autores: ONU.

Referencia: ONU (2020). *Informe de los Objetivos de Desarrollo Sostenible 2020*. https://www.un.org/sustainabledevelopment/es/progress-report/

▶ Te invitamos a explorar un estudio esencial sobre la Agenda 2030 para el Desarrollo Sostenible, un plan global iniciado en 2015 con la ambiciosa meta de erradicar la pobreza y promover la paz, la prosperidad y las oportunidades para todos en un planeta saludable. Con sus 17 Objetivos de Desarrollo Sostenible (ODS), esta agenda exige transformaciones profundas en nuestros sistemas financieros, económicos y políticos para garantizar los derechos humanos universales. Aunque hemos visto avances, como la reducción del abandono escolar y mejoras en el acceso al agua potable, la pandemia de COVID-19 ha ampliado las desigualdades existentes, afectando desproporcionadamente a los más vulnerables y ralentizando el progreso hacia estos objetivos. Este informe hace un llamado a una respuesta internacional coordinada que fortalezca los sistemas de salud, garantice el acceso universal a tratamientos y vacunas, y promueva una recuperación económica sostenible y equitativa.

Industry, Innovation, and Infrastructure Report 2021

Autores: ONU.

Referencia: ONU (2021). *Industry, Innovation, and Infrastructure Report 2021. Departamento de Asuntos Económicos y Sociales de las Naciones Unidas.* https://www.un.org/development/desa/dpad/publication/world-economic-situation-and-prospects-2021/

▶ Para saber más descubre un estudio esencial publicado por el Departamento de Asuntos Económicos y Sociales de las Naciones Unidas. Este informe examina el progreso y los desafíos relacionados con el Objetivo de Desarrollo Sostenible (ODS) 9, que se centra en desarrollar infraestructuras resilientes, promover la industrialización inclusiva y sostenible, y fomentar la innovación. Estos elementos son clave para alcanzar los objetivos de la Agenda 2030. Al comprender y apoyar estos pilares, podemos contribuir a construir un mundo más fuerte y equitativo para todos.

World Employment and Social Outlook – Trends 2021

Autores: Organización Internacional del Trabajo.

Referencia: Organización Internacional del Trabajo (2021). *World Employment and Social Outlook – Trends 2021*. https://www.oitcinterfor.org/en/node/8150

▶ Hoy quiero invitarte a explorar un informe crucial publicado por la Organización Internacional del Trabajo (OIT). Este estudio analiza las tendencias y desafíos globales en el empleo y las condiciones laborales, centrándose en el impacto que la pandemia de COVID-19 ha tenido en el trabajo decente y el crecimiento económico. A través de datos y análisis detallados, el informe nos muestra cómo los países pueden recuperarse y avanzar hacia el Objetivo de Desarrollo Sostenible (ODS) 8, que promueve el trabajo decente y el crecimiento económico sostenible.

Nuevos Escenarios Educativos

ESCENARIO EDUCATIVO dirigido a estudiantes

Taller de simulación logística con V-Logistics en la empresa

ODS vinculados

Actividad

La actividad consiste en un taller interactivo diseñado para estudiantes que tomarán el rol de personas empleadas de alguna empresa de comercio internacional. Desde ese rol harán uso de la plataforma V-Logistics que les permita simular escenarios de comercio internacional y operaciones aduaneras. La actividad tiene un enfoque lúdico y participativo para promover el aprendizaje y la cohesión del equipo.

Objetivo

Mejorar las habilidades logísticas y la toma de decisiones de cada participante, proporcionando una comprensión práctica del impacto de la logística en el comercio internacional y las operaciones aduaneras.

Inicio

1. Preparativos iniciales
   - Configuración técnica y prueba de la plataforma V-Logistics en el equipo de cómputo que se utilizará.
   - Distribución de materiales de apoyo a cada participante (manuales, guías, etc.).
2. Introducción al taller
   - Presentación del equipo facilitador y objetivos del taller.
   - Explicación de la dinámica del taller y la importancia de la simulación logística.
   - Breve introducción a la plataforma V-Logistics y sus funcionalidades.

Desarrollo

1. Primera fase - Introducción a la simulación
   - Explicación detallada de la plataforma y sus herramientas.
   - Asignación de roles y tareas dentro del entorno simulado, fomentando el trabajo en equipo.
2. Segunda fase - Ejecución de la simulación
   - Cada participante interactúa con la plataforma para gestionar operaciones logísticas y aduaneras.
   - Resolución de problemas y toma de decisiones en tiempo real, enfrentando escenarios simulados.
   - Incorporación de elementos lúdicos como retos y premios para motivar la participación activa.
3. Tercera fase - Evaluación y ajustes
   - Monitoreo de las decisiones y desempeño de cada participante.
   - Realización de ajustes y correcciones según el *feedback* instantáneo de la plataforma.

Cierre

1. Análisis y discusión
   - Sesión de debate y reflexión sobre las decisiones tomadas durante la simulación.
   - Evaluación de los resultados y comparación con escenarios reales.
2. Retroalimentación y conclusiones
   - Recopilación de opiniones y sugerencias de cada participante.
   - Resumen de los aprendizajes clave y cierre formal del taller.

Evaluación

- Cuestionarios de experiencia de usuario (UX) y eGame Flow (que están integrados en la plataforma v-Logistics).
- Evaluación de habilidades prácticas mediante observación directa y *feedback* de las personas facilitadoras.
- Análisis de decisiones tomadas y su impacto en la simulación.

Evidencia de aprendizaje

- Resultados de los cuestionarios UX y eGame Flow.
- Reportes de desempeño individual y grupal dentro de la plataforma.
- Registro de decisiones y sus consecuencias dentro de la simulación.

Materiales necesarios

- Acceso a computadoras con conexión a internet.
- Plataforma V-Logistics instalada y configurada.
- Materiales de apoyo (manuales, guías, presentaciones).
- Cuestionarios UX, eGame Flow, y eComplexity (Castillo-Martínez y Ramírez-Montoya, 2022).

Referencia

Castillo-Martínez, I. M. y Ramírez-Montoya, M. S. (2022). Instrumento eComplexity: Medición de la percepción de estudiantes de educación superior acerca de su competencia de razonamiento para la complejidad. https://hdl.handle.net/11285/643622

ESCENARIO EDUCATIVO dirigido a docentes

Laboratorio de acción para el aprendizaje en simulaciones

ODS vinculados

4 EDUCACIÓN DE CALIDAD

Actividad

Uso de la V-Logistics (plataforma educativa abierta que utiliza simulaciones y juegos serios) para fomentar el desarrollo de la competencia de pensamiento complejo y fomentar el aprendizaje autorregulado, a través de la resolución de problemas y toma de decisiones.

Objetivo

Crear una red logística para un emprendimiento donde cada participante tomará decisiones en escenarios seguros.

Inicio

Cada docente ofrecerá una breve introducción a la plataforma V-Logistics, destacando los objetivos de la actividad de laboratorio. Explicará cómo navegar por la plataforma y cómo utilizar las simulaciones y recursos disponibles.

Desarrollo

Cada participante explorará simulaciones que replican entornos empresariales y logísticos complejos. En estos escenarios seguros, podrán practicar la toma de decisiones con el objetivo de crear una red logística para un proyecto de educación abierta. Además, se facilitará el acceso a recursos educativos abiertos, como videos educativos, artículos informativos y cuestionarios, para profundizar en los conceptos de aprendizaje autorregulado y razonamiento para la complejidad. Esta actividad también promoverá el aprendizaje desde diversas perspectivas, integrando conocimientos de negocios, logística y educación abierta, ofreciendo así un enfoque multidisciplinario.

Cierre

Se realizará una sesión de cierre donde cada participante compartirá sus experiencias y aprendizajes. El cuerpo docente proporcionará retroalimentación y se fomentará una discusión reflexiva sobre las habilidades adquiridas.

Evaluación

El proceso de evaluación se podrá establecer a través de encuestas de retroalimentación por parte de cada participante, las observaciones de los facilitadores y los emprendimientos desarrollados.

La plataforma cuenta con instrumentos que permitirán valorar el nivel de percepción de pensamiento complejo, el aprendizaje autodirigido (*Self-directed Learning*), la experiencia de usuario (UX) y el flujo de juego (eGame Flow) una vez que se ha experimentado el uso de V-Logistics.

El cuestionario de eComplexity (Castillo-Martínez y Ramírez-Montoya, 2022) se aplica en dos momentos (pre-test y post-test) utilizando una escala Likert de autoevaluación del nivel de pensamiento complejo en cuatro dimensiones: complejo, sistémico, crítico e innovador, y mide conocimientos, habilidades y valores. De igual manera, se aplican los instrumentos de UX y eGame Flow para medir la experiencia del usuario y la experiencia de juego, respectivamente. Además, se utiliza un instrumento de aprendizaje autodirigido (pre-test y post-test), con una escala para evaluar la organización, gestión y solución de problemas en el aprendizaje.

Evidencia de Aprendizaje

Como evidencia de aprendizaje se retomarán los emprendimientos propuestos y desarrollados por cada participante, estos permitirán visualizar la comprensión y aplicación de los conocimientos adquiridos.

Materiales o Herramientas Digitales

- Plataforma de simulación S4L
- Recursos educativos abiertos (videos, artículos, cuestionarios)
- Herramientas de colaboración en línea (por ejemplo, Zoom, Microsoft Teams)

Referencia

Castillo-Martínez, I. M. y Ramírez-Montoya, M. S. (2022). Instrumento eComplexity: Medición de la percepción de estudiantes de educación superior acerca de su competencia de razonamiento para la complejidad. https://hdl.handle.net/11285/643622

ESCENARIO EDUCATIVO dirigido a empresas

Taller empresarial para el desarrollo de conceptos logísticos

ODS vinculados

8 TRABAJO DECENTE Y CRECIMIENTO ECONÓMICO

Actividad

Cada participante desarrollará habilidades para diseñar y optimizar redes logísticas mediante simulaciones y juegos educativos. Esta actividad utiliza simulaciones para enseñar sobre sistemas y procesos logísticos complejos, fomentando el pensamiento crítico y creativo.

Objetivo

Desarrollar la capacidad de cada participante para pensar de manera crítica y creativa sobre problemas complejos, así como aprender a identificar y aplicar soluciones adecuadas, a través de la caracterización de diferentes facilidades logísticas como pueden ser almacenes, centros de distribución y terminales de transporte.

Inicio

Cada participante se reunirá en un entorno virtual en el que recibirá una introducción de los conceptos clave de la logística y el uso de simulaciones como herramientas de aprendizaje. Se ofrece una breve introducción sobre la importancia de V-Logistics en términos de la flexibilidad y la facilidad de recrear diferentes escenarios logísticos.

Desarrollo

1. Ingresar a la página.
2. Leer el caso de estudio, Gaermont Sports, disponible en <https://medium.com/@ernesto1411/gaermont-sport-da9a1660b9c4>.
3. Las personas participantes trabajarán en grupos para resolver problemas logísticos, fomentando la colaboración y el desarrollo de habilidades blandas. Realizarán los ejercicios que se especifican en el caso de estudio.

Cierre

Cada grupo presentará sus soluciones a los problemas logísticos y recibirán retroalimentación de las personas encargadas de facilitar la actividad. Se llevará a cabo una discusión para consolidar el aprendizaje y reflexionar sobre las experiencias.

Evaluación

A partir de lo que se reconoció en el caso de estudio Gaermont Sports, se solicita a cada participante del área empresarial escribir y desarrollar un caso basándose en las características de su propia empresa.

Se utilizarán pruebas que están incorporadas en la plataforma antes y después de la actividad para medir el aprendizaje, encuestas de satisfacción, observaciones de las personas facilitadoras y estudios de caso desarrollados por cada participante. Instrumentos incorporados en plataforma: eComplexity (Castillo-Martínez y Ramírez-Montoya, 2022), Self-directed learning, User experience, eGame Flow.

Evidencia de Aprendizaje

Representar en el simulador el diseño de la cadena logística de su empresa. El escenario desarrollado debe corresponder a la narrativa de cada participante sobre el caso que han desarrollado.

Materiales o Herramientas Digitales

Herramientas de comunicación y colaboración en línea (por ejemplo, Zoom, Microsoft Teams)

Videos sobre el uso del editor o creador de juegos

- https://youtu.be/kPb3qPUIwuo
- https://youtu.be/1cP8yY_mZx0
- https://youtu.be/BuRBUQCh8gA
- https://youtu.be/cHoFPU9Gxzk
- https://youtu.be/TQLb-dMLDIw
- https://youtu.be/G280SI5Xrrs
- https://youtu.be/10qFkKKy0wU

Videos sobre el uso del simulador

- https://youtu.be/RCGIdSLcWTw
- https://youtu.be/gaNNQ5GZifo
- https://youtu.be/Z0Qe449BLMI
- https://youtu.be/qWselY_rzl0
- https://youtu.be/IPJoPd30NhQ

Referencia

Castillo-Martínez, I. M. y Ramírez-Montoya, M. S. (2022). Instrumento eComplexity: Medición de la percepción de estudiantes de educación superior acerca de su competencia de razonamiento para la complejidad. https://hdl.handle.net/11285/643622

ESCENARIO EDUCATIVO dirigido a ONG

Taller práctico de simulación logística con V-Logistics para mujeres emprendedoras

ODS vinculados

Actividad

Este taller dinámico sumerge a las mujeres del colectivo en la gestión logística mediante la plataforma V-Logistics. A través de simulaciones prácticas, fortalecen sus habilidades empresariales y estratégicas, preparándolas para desarrollar habilidades de liderazgo en un entorno empresarial globalizado y equitativo.

Objetivo

Desarrollar competencias a mujeres del colectivo en aspectos prácticos de la logística, facilitando su integración y liderazgo efectivo en el mundo empresarial.

Inicio

1. Preparación y bienvenida
   - Configuración inicial de la plataforma V-Logistics para una experiencia interactiva y educativa.
   - Presentación del equipo facilitador, destacando la relevancia estratégica de la logística en el desarrollo empresarial y la importancia de la participación femenina.
2. Introducción al taller
   - Sesión inicial sobre la importancia de la logística en la competitividad empresarial y oportunidades para mujeres emprendedoras.
3. Presentación del ejemplo de aplicación real
   - *Imagina a Lucía, una emprendedora que desea expandir su negocio de productos artesanales a mercados internacionales. Utilizando V-Logistics, Lucía aprende a optimizar sus procesos de envío y distribución, reduciendo costos y tiempos de entrega.*

Desarrollo

1. Capacitación práctica
   - Instrucción guiada sobre el uso de V-Logistics, explorando funciones clave para la gestión de cadenas de suministro y logística.
   - Ejemplos prácticos de aplicaciones empresariales con enfoque en desafíos logísticos reales.

   Presentación del ejemplo de aplicación real

   María, otra participante del taller, administra una pequeña empresa de alimentos saludables. A través de simulaciones, aprende a gestionar eficazmente la cadena de suministro desde la producción hasta la clientela final, mejorando la calidad del servicio y la satisfacción de su clientela.

Desarrollo *(continuación)*

2. Simulación empresarial
   - Implementación de simulaciones logísticas para resolver problemas como distribución eficiente, gestión de inventarios y optimización de rutas.
   - Trabajo en equipos para tomar decisiones estratégicas y enfrentar escenarios dinámicos.

   Presentación del ejemplo de aplicación real

   Ana, quien lidera un colectivo de mujeres productoras de artesanías locales, utiliza las simulaciones para coordinar la logística de exportación hacia nuevos mercados, garantizando la llegada oportuna de sus productos y cumpliendo con estándares internacionales de calidad.
3. Análisis y reflexión
   - Sesión de revisión post-simulación para discutir estrategias adoptadas, compartir aprendizajes clave y explorar aplicaciones prácticas en negocios reales.
   - Debate sobre la importancia de la logística en el éxito empresarial y la capacidad de las mujeres para liderar en este campo.

Cierre

1. Conclusiones y próximos pasos
   - Recapitulación de los logros individuales y grupales durante el taller.
   - Enfoque en la continuación del desarrollo personal y profesional en logística y estrategia empresarial.

   Presentación del ejemplo de aplicación real

   Después del taller, las participantes como Lucía, María y Ana implementan las estrategias aprendidas en sus negocios, observando mejoras significativas en eficiencia operativa y competitividad en el mercado global.
2. Impacto y seguimiento
   - Evaluación del impacto del taller en las habilidades logísticas y estratégicas de las participantes.
   - Recomendaciones para futuras actividades y programas de desarrollo empresarial dentro del colectivo, fortaleciendo la inclusión y liderazgo femenino en sectores estratégicos.

Evaluación

- Uso de cuestionarios adaptados de experiencia de usuario (UX) para medir la efectividad y satisfacción con V-Logistics.
- Evaluación de decisiones estratégicas tomadas durante las simulaciones mediante retroalimentación cualitativa y cuantitativa.
- Análisis del desarrollo de habilidades empresariales y estratégicas como evidencia de aprendizaje.

Materiales necesarios

- Acceso a computadoras con conexión a internet y configuración de V-Logistics.
- Guías prácticas y recursos digitales sobre logística empresarial y estrategia.

ESCENARIO EDUCATIVO dirigido a *lifelong learning*

Taller práctico de gamificación y juegos serios: aprendizaje a lo largo de la vida con V-Logistics

ODS vinculados

Actividad

Taller que utiliza la plataforma V-Logistics para introducir a cada participante en el mundo de la logística mediante juegos serios y gamificación. Se enfoca en el desarrollo de competencias clave para el aprendizaje continuo y el crecimiento profesional.

Objetivo

Fomentar el aprendizaje activo y continuo a través de juegos serios y gamificación, utilizando V-Logistics como herramienta principal para la simulación y gestión de cadenas logísticas.

Inicio

1. Bienvenida y presentación
   - Introducción al concepto de juegos serios y gamificación en el aprendizaje a lo largo de la vida.
   - Importancia de la logística en la economía global y el desarrollo profesional.

   Presentación de ejemplo de aplicación real

   Imagínate a Carlos, un profesional en crecimiento que desea mejorar sus habilidades logísticas para cumplir los objetivos en su carrera. A través de juegos serios en V-Logistics, Carlos aprende a optimizar rutas de distribución y mejorar la eficiencia operativa de su empresa.

Desarrollo

1. Capacitación práctica
   - Uso guiado de V-Logistics para simular situaciones reales de gestión logística.
   - Ejemplos prácticos de aplicación empresarial enfocados en desafíos logísticos globales.

   Presentación de ejemplo de aplicación real

   María, una emprendedora que gestiona una cadena de suministro local, utiliza las simulaciones para aprender estrategias de gestión de inventarios y optimización de costos, mejorando así la competitividad de su negocio en el mercado actual.
2. Simulación empresarial
   - Implementación de escenarios dinámicos para resolver problemas complejos de logística.
   - Trabajo en equipos para tomar decisiones estratégicas y enfrentar desafíos emergentes.

   Presentación de ejemplo de aplicación real

   Ana, una profesional en formación que colabora con una ONG local, utiliza V-Logistics para coordinar la distribución de recursos a comunidades remotas, mejorando la eficiencia y el impacto de las intervenciones humanitarias.

Desarrollo *(continuación)*

3. Análisis y reflexión
    - Sesión de revisión post-simulación para discutir estrategias efectivas y compartir aprendizajes significativos.
    - Debate sobre la aplicación de juegos serios en entornos educativos y profesionales.

Cierre

1. Conclusiones y próximos pasos
    - Evaluación de los logros individuales y grupales durante el taller.
    - Enfoque en la aplicación continua de habilidades adquiridas en la práctica profesional y educativa.

    Presentación de ejemplo de aplicación real

    Después del taller, las personas participantes como Carlos, María y Ana aplican las estrategias aprendidas en sus respectivos campos, observando mejoras tangibles en la eficiencia operativa y la toma de decisiones estratégicas.
2. Impacto y seguimiento
    - Evaluación del impacto de los juegos serios en el aprendizaje y desarrollo profesional.
    - Recomendaciones para futuras iniciativas de formación continua y educación gamificada.

Evaluación

- Uso de herramientas de evaluación adaptadas para medir la efectividad y el aprendizaje a través de juegos serios.
- Evaluación de competencias desarrolladas como evidencia de aprendizaje y progreso profesional.

Materiales o Herramientas Digitales

- Acceso a la plataforma V-Logistics y recursos educativos complementarios.
- Videos 360, infografías y guías prácticas para facilitar el aprendizaje continuo y autónomo.
- Materiales de apoyo y documentación para reforzar conceptos aprendidos durante el taller.

Este taller práctico de gamificación y juegos serios con V-Logistics no solo fortalece las competencias logísticas de cada participante, sino que también promueve el aprendizaje a lo largo de la vida de manera dinámica y efectiva. A través de simulaciones interactivas y trabajo colaborativo, profesionales y estudiantes pueden desarrollar habilidades esenciales para enfrentar los desafíos actuales del mercado global. Continuar con estas iniciativas no solo mejora la educación y el desarrollo profesional, sino que también contribuye al cumplimiento de los ODS, promoviendo una educación inclusiva, equitativa y de calidad para todas las personas.

Recomendaciones para la Implementación

La implementación de la plataforma V-Logistics debe adaptarse al grupo de interés en el que se vaya a utilizar. A continuación, se identifican los cuatro sectores clave y los beneficios específicos para cada uno de ellos (Figura 5).

Recomendaciones para implementar la plataforma S4L.

- **Academia:** fomenta competencias metacognitivas y pensamiento complejo a través de juegos serios y simulaciones.
- **Industria (pymes):** aborda desafíos de administración, conocimiento y tecnología con el simulador logístico V-Logistics.
- **Dependencias gubernamentales:** impulsa la resiliencia y el crecimiento sostenible frente a los retos de la industria 5.0, mejorando habilidades relevantes.
- **Sociedad Civil:** promueve el aprendizaje continuo y la conexión entre sectores para enfrentar las necesidades de la industria 5.0.

La plataforma V-Logistics ofrece un mapa de navegación con tres secciones de actividades principales, todas respaldadas por el editor y simulador logístico:

a) Construye tu red logística
b) Juegos gratis
c) Rutas de aprendizaje

Además, hay secciones complementarias para acceder al tablero de resultados, contactar al equipo, acceder a recursos educativos y leer testimonios de uso.

Contemplar los objetivos que tiene cada sección de la plataforma:

- **Construye tu red logística:** proporciona a cada participante un editor y simulador integrado para aplicar y experimentar con principios, decisiones y estrategias logísticas en un entorno controlado pero dinámico.

- **Juegos gratis:** comparte una variedad de juegos logísticos previamente creados, con la intención de enriquecer la experiencia práctica de cada persona usuaria de manera divertida y sin costo alguno. Estos juegos facilitan el aprendizaje interactivo y aplicado de temas en logística, operaciones y cadenas de suministro, promoviendo el desarrollo de competencias a través de la experimentación.

- **Rutas de aprendizaje:** guía al participante a través de una secuencia didáctica estructurada. Comienza con la autopercepción inicial de competencias como el pensamiento complejo y el aprendizaje autorregulado, y progresa a través de casos y ejercicios de simulación logística que permiten evaluar el desarrollo de estas competencias. También se valora la experiencia de juego y la experiencia de usuario, corroborando el desarrollo de competencias al final de la actividad mediante instrumentos específicos.

Preparación y bienvenida

Para garantizar el éxito de la implementación, es clave compartir de manera anticipada con cada participante un kit de bienvenida que incluya:

- Invitación a la actividad
- Registro en la plataforma
- Objetivos e intenciones
- Agenda
- Firma de consentimiento informado
- Acompañamiento de una persona facilitadora, ya sea en sala o en un entorno virtual

Además, es importante establecer las expectativas de alcance y logro para cada experiencia programada. La sección de rutas de aprendizaje es la única que permite mostrar un tablero de resultados y emitir constancias de participación digitales de manera automatizada.

Figura 5. Recomendaciones para implementar la plataforma S4L

Considerar la experiencia de usuarios

Como ejemplo de la captación de experiencia de usuarios y de la validación de la efectividad de la plataforma, se realizó un estudio piloto con 249 estudiantes de ocho universidades de cinco países latinoamericanos para evaluar la usabilidad de este generador de simulación en la educación en logística. El estudio reveló hallazgos importantes: (a) el generador de simulación brinda a los estudiantes experiencias educativas flexibles y personalizadas; (b) los aspectos de interfaz y rendimiento y efectividad de Virtual Logistics recibieron una calificación alta, alcanzando un nivel de usabilidad de "Bueno a Excelente":

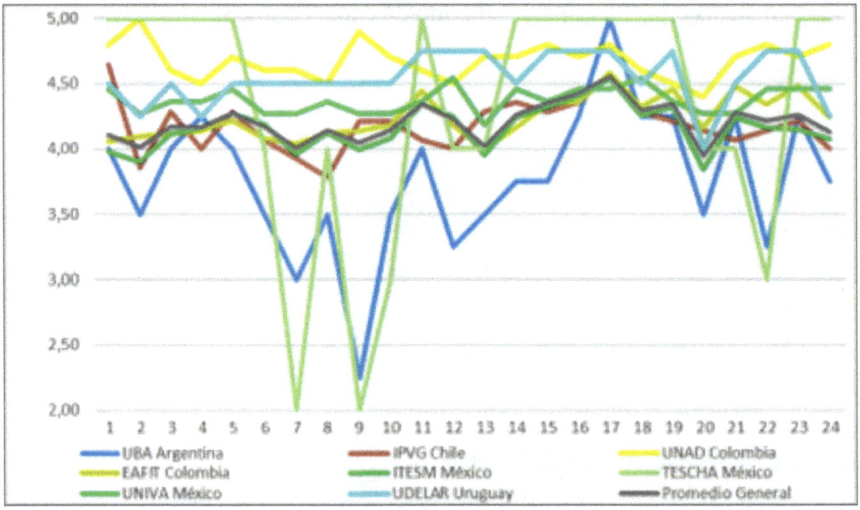

Informe general de usabilidad

Dimensión	Méritos	Nivel de usabilidad
Organización de contenidos	78,80 %	Bueno
Navegación	78,83 %	Bueno
Interfaz	82,98 %	Excelente
Rendimiento y eficacia	80,30 %	Excelente

Estos resultados demuestran la satisfacción de los estudiantes y, por lo tanto, el potencial transformador de las herramientas de aprendizaje basadas en simulación en la educación en logística. Virtual Logistics ofrece una valiosa guía para educadores, formuladores de políticas y líderes de la industria, alineando las herramientas educativas con los requisitos dinámicos, asegurando que los futuros profesionales estén bien equipados para enfrentar las complejidades del panorama logístico moderno.

Como ejemplo de aplicación en estudios de investigación, se aplicó el *serious game* a estudiantes del área de negocios, así como a estudiantes de programas de ingeniería industrial e ingeniería de producción (n=212, rango de evaluación: 0–7, siendo 7 excelencia).

Descripción de factores evaluados, medias y desviaciones estándar

Factor	Media	Desviación estándar
Concentración (C)	5.67	1.15
Claridad de objetivos (G)	5.98	1.21
Retroalimentación (F)	5.45	1.39
Desafío (H)	5.76	1.13
Autonomía (A)	6.00	0,91
Inmersión (I)	5.44	1.52
Interacción social (S)	5.54	1.35

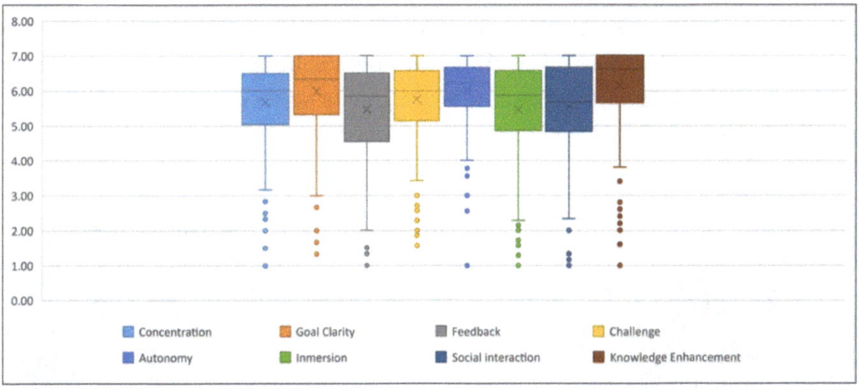

Implementación

Reporte de caso de éxito en Colombia

El lunes 30 de septiembre de 2024, el Dr. Ernesto Pacheco del Tecnológico de Monterrey implementó V-Logistics con colaboradores de la Universidad Nacional Abierta y a Distancia (UNAD) y de la Universidad Antonio Nariño (UAN), quienes actualmente tienen interés en incorporar el simulador asociándolo al programa académico de dos cursos que actualmente están siendo rediseñados.

Ellos se asociaron con un grupo de trabajo llamado Logyca que busca aportar valor a las compañías para su crecimiento y desarrollo partiendo del análisis de datos y la calidad de la información, y que genera conocimiento aplicable en la gestión de las redes de valor. Se hizo un recorrido en la empresa para conocer la cadena logística:

logyca

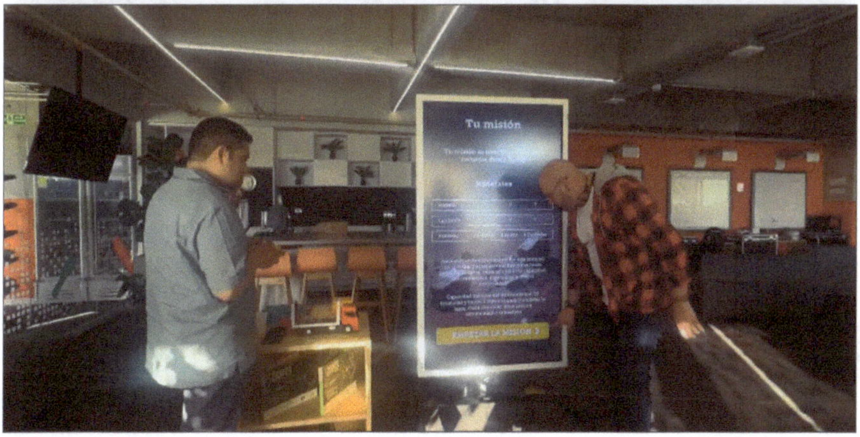
Tu misión

La validación de la efectividad de la plataforma V-Logistics es fundamental para asegurar que esta herramienta educativa cumple con su propósito de proporcionar una experiencia de aprendizaje práctica, inmersiva y alineada con las demandas reales del sector logístico. Evaluar su impacto en diferentes contextos académicos y profesionales no solo permite mejorar su funcionalidad y contenido, sino también fortalece su relevancia y aplicabilidad en la formación de habilidades clave como la toma de decisiones, la resolución de problemas y el pensamiento crítico. Al validar su efectividad, se confirma el valor de V-Logistics como un recurso esencial en la educación logística y en la preparación de estudiantes y profesionales para enfrentar con éxito los desafíos del entorno laboral actual.

RECURSOS EDUCATIVOS ABIERTOS (REA)

REA: V-Logistics Sesión 1. Introducción. Inicio de sesión.
Autor: Ernesto Armando Pacheco-Velázquez.
Referencia: Pacheco-Velázquez, E. A. (2024). *V-Logistics Sesión 1.* Introducción. Inicio de sesión [Infográfico]. https://repositorio.tec.mx/handle/11285/652417

▶ Iniciamos con un recurso educativo, en formato infográfico, que te ayudará a empezar con el pie derecho en tu curso de V-Logistics. Este infográfico te guía paso a paso sobre cómo iniciar sesión, brindándote un apoyo visual claro y directo para la primera sesión del curso. Imagina que estamos juntos, desentrañando cada detalle para que tu inicio sea sencillo y sin complicaciones. Esta herramienta visual es perfecta para asegurarte de que aproveches al máximo todo lo que V-Logistics tiene para ofrecer. Únete a esta experiencia de aprendizaje y hagamos juntos que tu viaje educativo sea fluido y exitoso. ¡Vamos a iniciar una gran aventura de aprendizaje!

REA: V-Logistics—Virtual platform for logistics learning.
Autor: Leonardo David Glasserman Morales.
Referencia: Glasserman Morales, L. D. (2024). *V-Logistics—Virtual platform for logistics learning* [Video]. https://hdl.handle.net/11285/676168

▶ Te invitamos a explorar un recurso educativo, en formato video, que presenta V-Logistics, un sistema de gestión de contenidos educativos (LCMS) que impulsa el pensamiento complejo y las competencias de aprendizaje autorregulado. Este sistema se basa en los avances de la industria 5.0, integrando inteligencia artificial, simulación, análisis de datos y recursos educativos abiertos. Todo esto con el objetivo de formar profesionales capaces de lograr un aprendizaje significativo y continuo a lo largo de sus vidas. Imagina que estamos juntos, explorando cómo V-Logistics puede revolucionar nuestra manera de aprender y enseñar, preparando a los estudiantes para enfrentar los desafíos del futuro con habilidades críticas y adaptativas. Únete a esta comunidad de aprendizaje y descubramos juntos el potencial de esta innovadora herramienta. ¡Vamos a aprender y crecer juntos!

REA: Jugando y aprendiendo: desarrollo de competencias para la vida.
Autores: Carolina Alcántar (entrevistadora), Azeneth Patiño y Leonardo Glasserman (entrevistados).
Referencia: Carolina Alcántar, C., Patiño, A. y Glasserman Morales, L. D. (2024). *Jugando y aprendiendo: desarrollo de competencias para la vida* [Video]. Programa de webcast: Futuro de la educación en la complejidad. Tecnológico de Monterrey. https://hdl.handle.net/11285/676178

▶ Te compartimos un recurso educativo, en formato de entrevista, titulado "Jugando y aprendiendo: desarrollo de competencias para la vida". En este fascinante webinar, Carolina Alcántar entrevista a dos especialistas, Azeneth Patiño y Leonardo Glasserman, quienes nos compartirán cómo los juegos serios pueden ser herramientas poderosas para el desarrollo de habilidades vitales. Imagínate que estamos todos juntos en esta conversación, descubriendo cómo estos recursos pueden mejorar el pensamiento complejo, la toma de decisiones, la resolución de problemas y la gestión del tiempo. Acompáñanos en esta exploración y veamos cómo jugar puede convertirse en una estrategia educativa efectiva. ¡Vamos a aprender de esta gran entrevista!

REA: Analizando las ventajas del uso de simuladores en educación logística.
Autores: Pamela Olivo (entrevistadora), Iván Andrés Arana González y Ricardo Thierry (entrevistados).
Referencia: Olivo, P., Arana González, I. A. y Thierry, R. (2024). Analizando las ventajas del uso de simuladores en educación logística [Video]. Programa de webcast: Futuro de la educación en la complejidad. Tecnológico de Monterrey. https://hdl.handle.net/11285/676179

▶ A través de un recurso educativo fascinante, en formato de entrevista, tenemos un webinar organizado por el proyecto S4L, titulado "Analizando las ventajas del uso de simuladores en educación logística", tendrás la oportunidad de descubrir cómo estas herramientas pueden revolucionar el aprendizaje en el campo de las cadenas de suministro. Imagina que estamos juntos escuchando a Pamela Olivo mientras entrevista a expertos como Iván Andrés Arana González y Ricardo Thierry. A lo largo de esta conversación, aprenderemos cómo los simuladores pueden proporcionar a los profesionales herramientas específicas para liderar estrategias de negocio e incorporar nuevos conocimientos en su práctica diaria. Acompáñanos en esta experiencia enriquecedora y descubramos juntos cómo mejorar nuestras habilidades logísticas. ¡Vamos a aprender sobre logística con expertos!

REA: Proposal for a Participatory Methodology for the Creation of Serious Games.
Autores: Ernesto Armando Pacheco-Velázquez, Lucia Rabago Mayer, Andre Bester y Virginia Rodés Paragarino.
Referencia: Pacheco-Velazquez, E. A., Bester, A., Rabago Mayer, L., y Rodes-Paragarino, V. (2023). Proposal for a Participatory Methodology for the Creation of Serious Games. En *European Conference on Games Based Learning 17*(1), 475–481. https://repositorio.tec.mx/handle/11285/653799

▶ Exploremos un recurso educativo, en formato texto, presentado en una conferencia internacional, que aborda un tema fascinante y muy actual. La tecnología ha cambiado la forma de relacionarse de las personas con el mundo y, en el ámbito educativo, se ve como una herramienta que facilita el aprendizaje y desarrolla habilidades. En este contexto, los simuladores y los juegos serios emergen como estrategias efectivas para facilitar el aprendizaje. Los beneficios de los juegos serios son evidentes: fomentan el pensamiento crítico, la creatividad, mejoran la capacidad de resolución de problemas y aumentan la retención de información. Sin embargo, estos juegos deben estar bien diseñados para mantener su atractivo y esencia lúdica. El artículo que te invito a leer discute la importancia de establecer especificaciones y requisitos claros antes de pasar a la fase de desarrollo, implementación o evaluación de estos juegos. Analiza cómo la falta de una metodología de diseño adecuada y la ambigüedad en los requisitos pueden afectar la eficacia de los juegos serios. Este recurso es crucial para entender cómo crear juegos educativos efectivos que realmente impacten en el aprendizaje de los estudiantes. ¡Vamos a descubrir juntos cómo la tecnología puede transformar la educación!

LLAMADO A LA ACCIÓN

¡Nos encantaría escucharte y aprender juntos!
Los desafíos de nuestro tiempo solo pueden ser superados con colaboración y aprovechando el valor de la diversidad. Por eso, te invitamos a participar en el proyecto revisando la sección de contacto en el siguiente enlace de la plataforma V-Logistics: https://v-logistics.co/contact-us. Si tienes proyectos que quieras explorar, investigaciones que realizar, ideas para desarrollar o deseas capacitar a tu comunidad, estamos aquí para apoyarte. Queremos construir de manera colaborativa contigo, ya seas parte de la sociedad civil, escuelas, universidades, empresas o grupos tomadores de decisiones. Cada sector tiene una perspectiva única y valiosa que aportar al futuro de la educación.

¡Únete a nosotros y construyamos juntos un mejor futuro!
Nuestro grupo de investigación: https://tec.mx/es/r4c-irg
Explora nuestros proyectos: https://www.research4challenges.world/

Únete al proyecto V-Logistics:
https://www.research4challenges.world/s4l-1

GLOSARIO

Logística. La logística es el proceso de mover y almacenar productos desde donde se hacen hasta donde se necesitan. Esto incluye actividades como transportar, almacenar y gestionar inventarios para asegurarse de que los productos lleguen a los clientes de manera eficiente.

Cadena de suministro. La cadena de suministro es el conjunto de organizaciones y etapas que sigue un producto desde que se obtiene la materia prima hasta que llega al cliente final. Esto incluye la producción, almacenamiento, distribución y entrega del producto, asegurando que todo funcione de manera coordinada para satisfacer la demanda del consumidor.

Objetivos de Desarrollo Sostenible (ODS). Los ODS son un conjunto de metas globales y concretas orientadas a la acción, cuyo propósito es proteger el planeta, erradicar la pobreza y alcanzar la paz y la prosperidad para todas las personas. Cada ODS incluye diversas metas específicas que detallan cómo lograr cada objetivo, promoviendo un enfoque integral para el desarrollo sostenible en todo el mundo.

Pensamiento complejo. El pensamiento complejo es la competencia de observar la realidad considerando la totalidad de los factores que convergen para darle forma. En lugar de enfocarse en cada factor de manera aislada, se entiende que cada parte contribuye y es influida por la totalidad de la realidad. Este enfoque integrador permite comprender cómo las diferentes partes se interrelacionan y afectan mutuamente, proporcionando una visión más completa y profunda del mundo.

Futuro de la Educación – Future of Education

Edited by María Soledad Ramírez-Montoya, Rasikh Tariq, Leonardo David Glasserman Morales, Edgar Omar López-Caudana & Inés Alvarez-Icaza Longoria

VOL. 1 María Soledad Ramírez-Montoya, Edgar Omar López-Caudana, Inés Alvarez-Icaza Longoria, Carlos Vásquez-Parra, Fabian Eduardo Basabe, Carolina Alcántar-Nieblas, Pamela Geraldine Olivo Montaño, Virginia Rodés Paragarino, Isolda Margarita Castillo-Martínez, Laura Icela González-Pérez & May Portuguez Castro: Mobilise Your Thinking for Complexity. Open Educational Model for Complex Thinking – Moviliza tu Pensamiento para la Complejidad. Modelo Educativo Abierto para el Pensamiento Complejo. 2026.

VOL. 2 María Soledad Ramírez-Montoya, Edgar Omar López-Caudana, Inés Alvarez-Icaza Longoria, Carlos Enrique George Reyes, Paloma Suárez Brito & Pamela Geraldine Olivo Montaño: Education 5.0 to mobilise social, scientific and technological entrepreneurship. OpenEdR4C Platform – Educación 5.0 para movilizar emprendimiento social, científico y tecnológico. Plataforma OpenEdR4C. 2026.

VOL. 3 María Soledad Ramírez-Montoya, Rasikh Tariq, Edgar Omar López-Caudana, José Martín Molina Espinosa, Miguel González Mendoza, Carlos Enrique George Reyes, Magally Martínez Reyes, Irma Azeneth Patiño Zúñiga, Paloma Suárez Brito & Pamela Geraldine Olivo Montaño: Boost Your Computational and Complex Thinking. E4C&CT Digital Ecosystem Platform – Impulsa tu Pensamiento Computacional y Razonamiento Complejo. Plataforma de ecosistema digital E4C&CT. 2026.

VOL. 4 María Soledad Ramírez-Montoya, Ernesto Armando Pacheco-Velázquez, Leonardo David Glasserman Morales, Virginia Rodés Paragarino, Carolina Alcántar-Nieblas, Pamela Geraldine Olivo Montaño & Fidel Antonio Guadalupe Casillas Muñoz: Let's Learn Logistics Through Simulation. S4L Platform – Aprendamos Logística a Través de la Simulación. Plataforma S4L. 2026.

www.peterlang.com

Printed by
CPI books GmbH, Leck